C000183142

PRACTICE
MAKES
PERFECT

Interactive

Beginning
Chinese

LiveABC

Mc Graw Hill

New York   Chicago   San Francisco   Lisbon   London   Madrid   Mexico City
Milan   New Delhi   San Juan   Seoul   Singapore   Sydney   Toronto

Copyright © 2009 by Live ABC. All rights reserved. Printed in China. Except as permitted under the United States Copyright Act of 1976, no part of this publication may be reproduced or distributed in any form or by any means, or stored in a database or retrieval system, without the prior written permission of the publisher.

4 5 6 7 8 9 10 11 12 13 14 15 16 17 18 19 20 21   CTP/CTP   14

ISBN 978-0-07-160412-3 (book and CD-ROM set)
MHID   0-07-160412-X (book and CD-ROM set)

ISBN 978-0-07160413-0 (book for set)
MHID   0-07160413-8 (book for set)

Library of Congress Control Number: 2008925290

Please see the final page of the book for instructions on loading the CD-ROM.

McGraw-Hill books are available at special quantity discounts to use as premiums and sales promotions or for use in corporate training programs. To contact a representative, please visit the Contact Us pages at www.mhprofessional.com.

This book is printed on acid-free paper.

Contents

家 & 高

How to Use This Book

Please note the following:

1. This publication is based on standard Chinese. For specific terms, it occasionally supplements other usages from China, Taiwan, or Hong Kong.

2. The content and vocabulary are chosen to meet the threshold level of the Hanyu Shuiping Kaoshi (Chinese proficiency test).

3. Pinyin is spelled according to the *Basic Rules for Hanyu Pinyin Orthography* and *INHUA PINXIE CIDIAN* (《新华拼写辞典》).

4. Grammar terms that specifically relate to Chinese are also used. Abbreviations for these terms are listed in the table on the right.

adv.	Adverb
ce.	Common Expression
conj.	Conjunction
interj.	Interjection
m.	Measure Word
n.	Noun
nu.	Numeral
p.	Particle
prep.	Preposition
pron.	Pronoun
qw.	Question Word
sv.	Stative Verb
t.	Time Word
v.	Verb

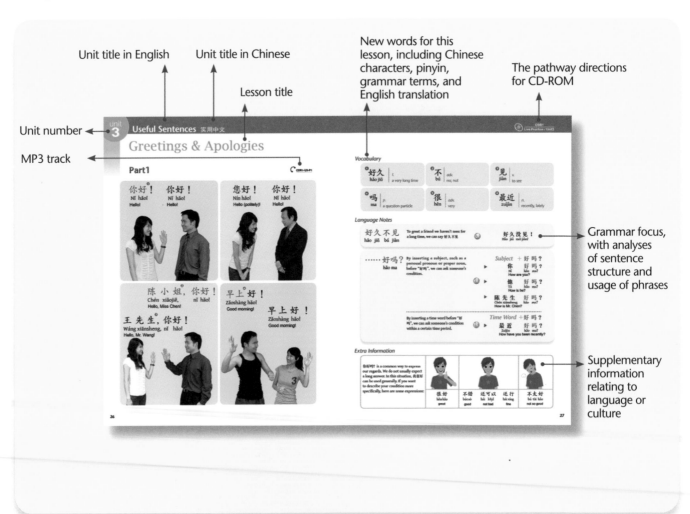

Unit title in English

Unit title in Chinese

Lesson title

New words for this lesson, including Chinese characters, pinyin, grammar terms, and English translation

The pathway directions for CD-ROM

Unit number

MP3 track

Grammar focus, with analyses of sentence structure and usage of phrases

Supplementary information relating to language or culture

How to Use the CD-ROM

System Requirements:

- Intel Pentium 4 CPU required
- Operation System: Windows XP and Vista or above
  (The speech recognition engine will not function under
  the Windows VISTA system.)
- 256 MB RAM (512 MB recommended)

- CD-ROM Drive
- High-Color Display: 16-bit color or above
- Sound Card, Speaker, and Microphone
- 500 MB of available hard-disk space
- Microsoft Media Player 9.0 or above

Listening to MP3 Files:

Our Interactive CD-ROM also includes MP3 files. You can listen to them either with your MP3 player or your computer. They are saved in the "MP3" directory.

Main Menu

Lessons on the CD-ROM are classified as Fun with Pronunciation, Conversation Classroom, Cultural Plaza, and Live Practice. They are followed by a Chinese Proficiency Test exercise and Role-Play activities. The Vocabulary Index includes a vocabulary glossary.

Review

Vocabulary Index

Chinese Pronunciation

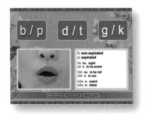

Conversation Classroom

Cultural Plaza

Video Mode

The video mode provides situational images that help learners put the lesson into context. With the video control functions, learners will not only enjoy the story but also practice listening. Learners are advised to follow three steps:

Step 1 Watch the video, enabling both Chinese and English subtitles.
Step 2 Turn the English subtitles off to focus on the Chinese.
Step 3 Turn both the English and Chinese subtitles off to test listening skills.

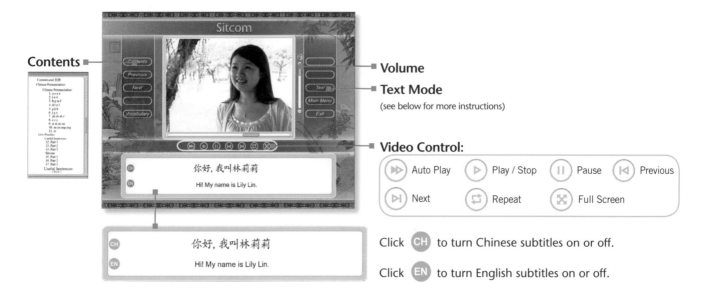

Contents

Volume

Text Mode

(see below for more instructions)

Video Control:

▶▶ Auto Play   ▶ Play / Stop   ❙❙ Pause   ◀❙ Previous

▶❙ Next   ⟲ Repeat   ✕ Full Screen

Click **CH** to turn Chinese subtitles on or off.

Click **EN** to turn English subtitles on or off.

你好, 我叫林莉莉
Hi! My name is Lily Lin.

你好, 我叫林莉莉
Hi! My name is Lily Lin.

Text Mode

This mode focuses on the text aspect of the dialogues. Multiple functions, such as Role-Play, Translate, Record, and Dictionary help learners to better understand Chinese. The text mode takes a new and dynamic approach in encouraging learners to practice reading and speaking.

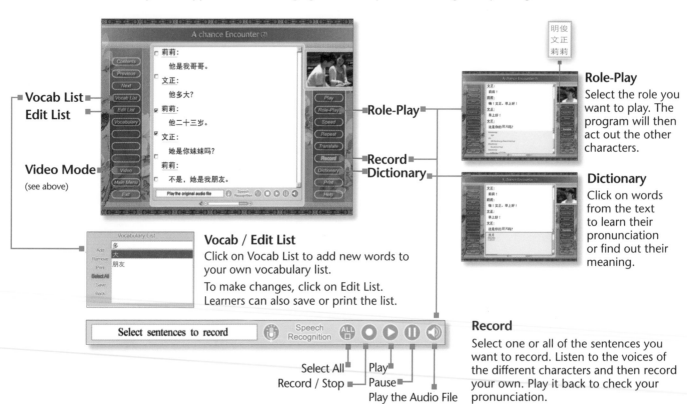

Vocab List
Edit List

Video Mode
(see above)

Role-Play

Record
Dictionary

Role-Play

Select the role you want to play. The program will then act out the other characters.

Dictionary

Click on words from the text to learn their pronunciation or find out their meaning.

Vocab / Edit List

Click on Vocab List to add new words to your own vocabulary list.

To make changes, click on Edit List. Learners can also save or print the list.

Select sentences to record   Speech Recognition

Select All
Record / Stop
Play
Pause
Play the Audio File

Record

Select one or all of the sentences you want to record. Listen to the voices of the different characters and then record your own. Play it back to check your pronunciation.

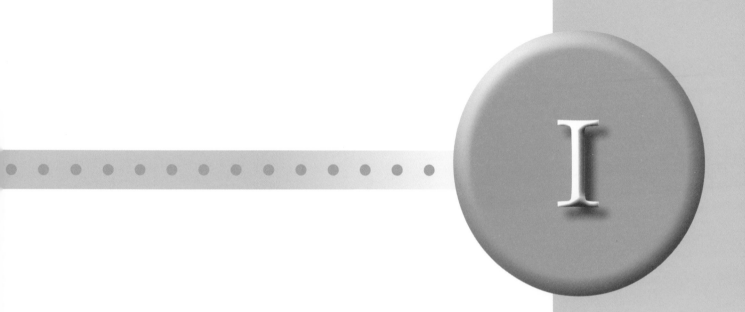

Chinese Pronunciation

 CDR1 - U1-P1

1 Basic construction of a Chinese syllable: initial + final + tone

2 Tones are the most remarkable characteristic of the Chinese language. There are five tones in Mandarin:

Tone	Tone mark	Pronouncing method	Example	
First tone	—		mā (n. mother)	
Second tone	╱		má (n. hemp)	
Third tone	∨		mǎ (n. horse)	
Fourth tone	╲		mà (v. to scold)	
Neutral tone			māma (n. mother)	

Note: Distinguishing between the tones is very important when you speak Chinese. The same syllable with a different tone likely has a different meaning. For beginners, the tones are quite tricky. However, it is the tones that make Chinese sound melodic. Try the following sentence to practice the tones:

Māma qí mǎ, mǎ màn, māma mà mǎ.

(Mother is riding a horse. The horse walks slowly so mother scolds the horse.)

Part 1

Simple Finals:

"a, o, e, ê, i, u, ü" are simple finals. They function like English vowels. When pronouncing these sounds, remember to focus on your mouth and tongue.

* Open your mouth naturally wide and keep your tongue in a flat, relaxed position.
* as in w**a**tch

| bàba | n. father |
| māma | n. mother |

* Make your mouth round and hold your tongue in the middle.
* This final does not have a corresponding English vowel sound.

| pópo | n. husband's mother |
| bóbo | n. father's elder brother |

* Open your mouth half-wide. At the same time, spread your lips apart, as if you were smiling.
* as in sev**e**n

| hē | v. to drink |
| kělè | n. cola |

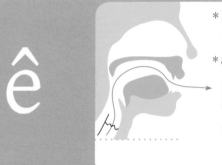

* Lower your tongue and keep your mouth flat, even flatter than when pronouncing the **e** sound.

* as in **e**gg

Ex.
xiě	v.	to write
xuě	n.	snow

Note: The **ê** sound doesn't exist on its own. It only appears with the finals **i** and **ü**, becoming the combinations **ie** and **üe**. In this situation, use the symbol **e**, instead of **ê**.

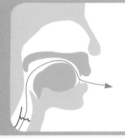

* Keep your mouth flat as if you were pronouncing the letter E.

* as in mach**i**ne

Ex.
nǐ	pron.	you
yī	nu.	one

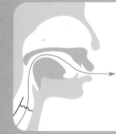

* Round your lips as if you were pronouncing "oo" in English.

* as in r**u**le

Ex.
bù	adv.	no; not
wǔ	nu.	five

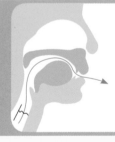

* First pronounce **i**. Then modify the shape of your mouth from an un-rounded position to rounded one.

* no English equivalent (like the German **ü**)

Ex.
nǚ	n.	female
yú	n.	fish

Note: If there is no initial before i, u, ü, they are spelled yi, wu, yu.

4

Part 2

Initials:

Initials function like English consonants. Many initials are pronounced approximately the same as their English counterparts, but watch out for "j, q, x, zh, ch, sh, r, z, c" as their pronunciations are very different.

1 Labial:

* Shut the lips tight enough to obstruct the air. Then open them to let out the air. This sound is not aspirated.
* as in **b**ay

EX.	bā	nu.	eight
	bǐ	n.	pencil

* Like **b**, the lips are shut tightly to obstruct the air. Open them quickly and force the air out. This sound is aspirated.
* as in **p**ay

EX.	pà	v.	to be afraid
	píjiǔ	n.	beer

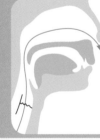

* Shut the lips tightly. Then let air out through the nasal cavity.
* as in **m**ay

EX.	mǎ	n.	horse
	míngzi	n.	name

* Press the upper teeth against the lower lip. Let out a breath. The sound relies on friction between the teeth and the lip.
* as in **f**at

EX.	fēijī	n.	airplane
	fàn	n.	rice

5

❷ Alveolar:

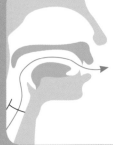

* Touch the tip of the tongue to the upper ridge of the teeth. Drop the tongue to let out the air. This sound is not aspirated.

* as in **d**ad

dà	sv.	to be big
dìdi	n.	younger brother

* Like **d**, the tip of the tongue touches the upper ridge of the teeth. Drop the tongue quickly to force the air out. This sound is aspirated.

* as in **t**ime

tā	pron.	he; him
tī	v.	to kick

* Touch the tip of the tongue to the upper ridge of the teeth. Let the air out through the nasal cavity.

* as in **n**urse

nà	pron.	that
nín	pron.	you (politely)

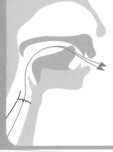

* Touch the tip of the tongue to the back of the upper ridge of the teeth. Let the air out from both sides of the tongue.

* as in **l**ion

lǐwù	n.	gift
kuàilè	sv.	to be happy

❸ Velar:

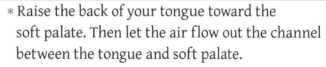

g

* Raise the back of your tongue against the soft palate. Then let out the air. This sound is not aspirated.
* as in **g**old

Ex.	gēge	n.	older brother
	gǒu	n.	dog

k

* As with **g**, put the back of your tongue against the soft palate. Then let the air out, only this time with a bit more force. This sound is aspirated.
* as in **k**ite

Ex.	kě	sv.	to be thirsty
	kū	v.	to cry

h

* Raise the back of your tongue toward the soft palate. Then let the air flow out the channel between the tongue and soft palate.
* as in **h**appy

Ex.	hěn	adv.	very
	hànyǔ	n.	Chinese (language)

Chinese Pronunciation 中文发音

④ Palatal:

* Raise the front of your tongue to the hard palate and press the tip against the back of the lower teeth. Then squeeze air out through the channel just formed. This sound is not aspirated.

* as in *jeep*

Ex.			
jiào	v.	to call, to be called
jùzi	n.	sentence

* As with **j**, raise the front of your tongue to the hard palate and press the tip against the back of the lower teeth. Then let the air out, but with greater force. This sound is aspirated.

* as in *cheer*

Ex.			
qī	nu.	seven
qù	v.	to go

* Raise the front of your tongue toward the hard palate. Then let the air flow out through the channel formed between your tongue and hard palate.

* as in *she*

Ex.			
xiǎo	sv.	to be small
xūyào	v.	to need

Note: 1. The pronunciation of j, q, x is different from their English counterparts. Remember to distinguish them.

2. j, q, x are always followed by the simple finals i and ü. When they are followed by ü, the two dots over ü can be omitted. The spellings become ju, qu, xu. However, they are still pronounced as ü.

❺Blade palatal:

zh

* Turn up the tip of your tongue against the hard palate. Then loosen it a bit to let out the air. This sound is not aspirated.
* as in *junk*

Ex.	zhè	*pron.*	this
	zhīdào	*v.*	to know

ch

* Like **zh**, turn up the tip of your tongue against the hard palate. Then loosen it a bit to let the air out, only with greater force. This sound is aspirated.
* as in **ch**urch

Ex.	chá	*n.*	tea
	chī	*v.*	to eat

sh

* Turn the tip of your tongue up toward the hard palate. Then let the air squeeze out.
* as in **sh**irt

Ex.	shénme	*qw.*	what
	shí	*nu.*	ten

r

* Turn the tip of your tongue up toward the hard palate to obstruct the breath. Then squeeze the air out.
* as in *r*abbit

Ex.	rén	*n.*	person, people
	rì	*n.*	day

Note: When zh, ch, sh, r appear alone, they are spelled zhi, chi, shi, ri.

⑥Blade alveolar: Z C S

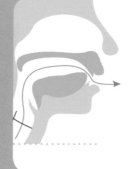

Z

* Place the tip of your tongue against the back of your teeth. Then let the air squeeze out between your tongue and teeth. This sound is not aspirated.
* as in ki**ds**

Ex.	zàijiàn	ce.	good-bye
	zì	n.	word

C

* As with **z**, place the tip of your tongue against the back of your teeth. Then let the breath out, only stronger, through the channel between your tongue and teeth. This sound is aspirated.
* as in ca**ts**

Ex.	cài	n.	dish
	cì	m.	time

S

* Place the tip of your tongue against the, back of your teeth. Then let the air out between your tongue and teeth, as if you were pronouncing the **s** sound in English.
* as in **s**ay

Ex.	sān	nu.	three
	sì	nu.	four

Note: 1. When z, c, s appear alone, they are spelled zi, ci, si.
     2. The difference between zh, ch, sh, r and z, c, s is in whether you roll your tongue or not. You do so when pronouncing zh, ch, sh, r. Do not roll your tongue when pronouncing z, c, s.

Extra Information

Some Chinese initials are aspirated and some are not, as you can see from the explanations just given. To see the difference more clearly, hold a piece of tissue in front of your mouth. When you pronounce a sound that is not aspirated, such as b, d, g, j, zh, z, the paper will remain still. When you pronounce an aspirated sound, such as p, t, k, q, ch, c, the paper will vibrate lightly. Take out a piece of tissue and practice.

Not aspirated   **Aspirated**

 Ex. b, d, g, j, zh, z   Ex. p, t, k, q, ch, c

Part 3

Compound Finals:

Compound finals combine two simple finals. When pronouncing them, the shape of the mouth and position of the tongue gradually change while the flow of air continues. Compound finals sound like one syllable.

ai

* **ai** consists of **a** and **i**. To pronounce **ai**, open your mouth and say **a** first. Then close it a bit to pronounce **i**.
* as in *kind*

Ex.			
	ài	*v.*	to love
	hǎi	*n.*	sea

ei

* **ei** consists of **e** and **i**. To pronounce **ei**, say **e** first. Then make your mouth flat to say **i**.
* as in *veil*

Ex.			
	hēi	*sv.*	to be black
	měi	*sv.*	to be beautiful

ao

* **ao** consists of **a** and **o**. To pronounce **ao**, open your mouth and say **a** first. Then round your mouth to say **o**.
* as in *sour*

Ex.			
	hǎo	*sv.*	to be good
	gāo	*sv.*	to be tall; to be high

ou

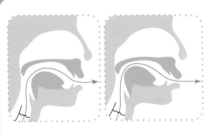

* **ou** consists of **o** and **u**. To pronounce **ou**, round your mouth and say **o** first. Then make your mouth even smaller to say **u**.
* as in *low*

Ex.			
	dōu	*adv.*	all
	tóu	*n.*	head

11

Part 4

Nasal Finals: **an** **en** **ang** **eng**

Nasal finals have nasal endings. Both an and en end with the n sound, which uses the front part of the nasal cavity, whereas ang and eng end with the ng sound, which uses the back part of the nasal cavity.

an

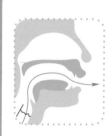 

* Open your mouth and say **a** first. Then close it a bit to let the air out through the nasal cavity ending with **n**.

* as in **aun**t

Ex.			
	àn	sv.	to be dark
	pánzi	n.	dish

en

* Keep your mouth flat to say **e** first. Then close it a bit to let the air out through the nasal cavity ending with **n**.

* as in Ry**an**

Ex.			
	mén	n.	door
	hěn	adv.	very

ang

* Open your mouth and say **a** first. Then let the air out through the back part of the nasal cavity ending with **ng**.

* as in h**ung**

Ex.			
	máng	sv.	to be busy
	cháng	sv.	to be long

eng

* Keep your mouth flat to say **e** first. Then close it a bit to let the air out through the back part of the nasal cavity ending with **ng**.

* as in the pronunciation of the letters "**uhng**" (uh-ng).

Ex.			
	fēng	n.	wind
	lěng	sv.	to be cold

Part 5

Retroflex:

* Turn up the tip of your tongue toward the hard palate. Then let the air out with your tongue rolled.

* as in *rear*

Ex.			
	èr	*nu.*	two
	yìdiǎnr	*adv.*	a little bit

Note: er is a special final and exists on its own. It can combine with other finals, however, to form a syllable with a retroflex ending. In this situation, r is added after a final that does not have e.

Part 6

Finals beginning with i, u, and ü:

Finals beginning with i, u, ü are created using a combination of i, u, ü and other finals. You should pronounce them in a way similar to how you pronounce compound finals. Some of the spellings are simplified, which may not represent their actual pronunciation (marked by ✱). Please pay special attention to these.

Finals	i	u	ü
a	ia	ua	
o		uo	
ê	ie		üe
ai		uai	
ei		ui*	
ao	iao		
ou	iu*		
an	ian	uan	üan
en	in*	un*	ün
ang	iang	uang	
eng	ing*	ong*	iong*

Note: In pinyin, if there is no initial before finals that begin with i, u, and ü, the general spelling rule is as follows: i⊠y, u⊠w, ü⊠yu. Please refer to the following form:

Without initial letters	With initial letters
iu	you
in	yin
ing	ying
ui	wei
ong	weng
iong	yong

13

Exercises

Listening

1. Listen to the recording and pronounce the words you hear. Then write down their phonetic spellings with the correct tone mark.

Ex. ____m____ ao

(1) _____ ǒu

(2) y_____

(3) sh _____

(4) _____ ǎn

(5) b _____

(6) h _____

(7) c _____

(8) sh _____

2. Listen to the recording file and distinguish the phonetic initials of each pair. If their initials have the same pronunciation, circle "Yes." Otherwise, circle "No."

Ex.   Yes   (No)

(1) Yes   No   (2) Yes   No   (3) Yes   No

(4) Yes   No   (5) Yes   No   (6) Yes   No

3. Listen to the recording and write the correct tone mark in the box.

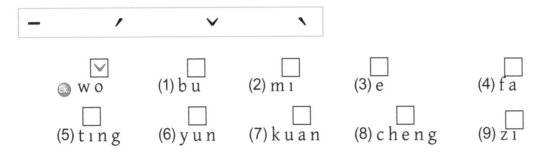

| ─ | ╱ | ╲ | ╲ |

Ex. w o [✓]

(1) b u [ ]

(2) m ı [ ]

(3) e [ ]

(4) f a [ ]

(5) t ı n g [ ]

(6) y u n [ ]

(7) k u a n [ ]

(8) c h e n g [ ]

(9) z ı [ ]

Activity

Listen to the recording and try to read the tongue twister.

老师爱书怕老鼠，
Lǎoshī ài shū pà lǎoshǔ,

The teacher loves books and is afraid of the mouse.

老鼠咬书怕老师，
Lǎoshǔ yǎo shū pà lǎoshī,

The mouse bites the book and is afraid of the teacher.

书爱老师怕老鼠。
Shū ài lǎoshī pà lǎoshǔ.

The book loves the teacher but is afraid of the mouse.

老师看书
Lǎoshī kàn shū

The teacher reads a book

最怕老鼠来咬书。
zuì pà lǎoshǔ lái yǎo shū.

and is most afraid of the mouse biting the book.

老鼠咬书
Lǎoshǔ yǎo shū

The mouse bites the book

最怕老师来看书。
zuì pà lǎoshī lái kàn shū.

and is most afraid of the teacher reading the book.

Personal Pronouns

Personal pronouns in Chinese can be used as a subject or object. There is, however, a small difference between singular and plural pronouns. Luckily, it's not complicated. Just follow our illustrations and you'll get it easily!

Singular

我
wǒ | *pron.* | I; me

你
nǐ | *pron.* | you

您
Nín | The polite form of you is 您. We usually use 您 to address the elderly, our superiors, or any other people we respect.

他
tā | *pron.* | he; him

她
tā | *pron.* | she; her

它
tā | *pron.* | it

他 (tā) usually means "he." If the gender is not emphasized or is unknown, 他 (tā) can indicate both "he" and "she. "她 (tā), on the other hand, can only mean "she." 它 (tā), like "it" in English, refers to an animal or item. Although 他, 她, and 它 are all pronounced "tā," the objects they refer to are different. Since all three characters sound the same, we don't need to worry about this when speaking.

Plural

To make singular personal pronouns plural, just add 们 (men) after 我 (wǒ), 你 (nǐ), 他(tā).
们 is used to refer to a group of two or more people.

我们 | *pron.*
wǒmen | we; us

你们 | *pron.*
nǐmen | you

他们 | *pron.*
tāmen | they; them

她们 | *pron.*
tāmen | they; them (referring to female only)

它们 | *pron.*
tāmen | they; them (referring to things and animals)

Interrogative

谁 | *qw.*
Shéi | who

To find out a person's identity, we can use the question word 谁 (shéi). For example, we can ask, "他是谁? (Tā shì shéi? Who is he?)" or "他们是谁? (Tāmen shì shéi? Who are they?)" when we want to know who somene is.

Exercises

Choice

Please read the sentences and look at the pictures. Choose the answer that matches the underlined word in the sentence.

☐ (1) <u>I</u> am a lady.

     a.我   b.你   c.他
      wǒ   nǐ   tā

☐ (2) <u>He</u> is my father. He is a doctor.

     a.她   b.你   c.他
      tā   nǐ   tā

☐ (3) Yesterday was my birthday. My sister gave <u>me</u> a gift.

     a.你   b.我   c.它
      nǐ   wǒ   tā

☐ (4) My birthday gift is a book. <u>It</u> is my favorite gift.

     a.你   b.我   c.它
      nǐ   wǒ   tā

☐ (5) Amy and her friends often go to karaoke. <u>They</u> love to sing.

     a.她们   b.你们   c.我 们
     tāmen   nǐmen   wǒmen

(6) Tony and Brain are neighbors. <u>They</u> love to play chess.

    a. 我 们   b. 你 们   c. 他 们
      wǒmen   nǐmen   tāmen

(7) Tom is my coworker. <u>We</u> are good friends.

    a. 你 们   b. 他 们   c. 我 们
      nǐmen   tāmen   wǒmen

(8) Tomorrow is Valentine's Day. Mary is Tom's girlfriend. Tom will give <u>her</u> some flowers.

    a. 他   b. 它   c. 她
      tā   tā   tā

(9) Today is the commencement at National Taiwan University. Tom, Amy, Annie, and Mary are graduating. <u>They</u> are happy.

    a. 她 们   b. 他 们   c. 我 们
      tāmen   tāmen   wǒmen

(10) Annie's teacher, Mr. Chen, gives her her diploma. Annie says: "Thank <u>you</u>" to Mr. Chen.

    a. 您   b. 我   c. 她
      nín   wǒ   tā

Greetings & Apologies

Part 1

你好❶!　你好!
Nǐ hǎo!　　Nǐ hǎo!
Hello!　　　Hello!

您好!　　　你好!
Nín hǎo!　　Nǐ hǎo!
Hello (politely)!　Hello!

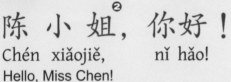

陈 小 姐❷，你好!
Chén xiǎojiě, nǐ hǎo!
Hello, Miss Chen!

王 先 生❸，你好!
Wáng xiānsheng, nǐ hǎo!
Hello, Mr. Wang!

早上❹好!
Zǎoshàng hǎo!
Good morning!

早上 好!
Zǎoshàng hǎo!
Good morning!

Vocabulary

❶ 好
hǎo | *sv.*
to be good

❷ 小姐
xiǎojiě | *n.*
Miss

❸ 先生
xiānsheng | *n.*
Mr.

❹ 早上
zǎoshàng | *n.*
morning

Language Notes

你好
nǐ hǎo
This is the most common greeting, meaning "hi" or "hello" in English. For greeting the elderly, we show respect by using: 您好！
Nín hǎo!

陈 小 姐 ， 你 好 ！
Chén xiǎojiě,　　nǐ hǎo!
Inserting a title before the greeting is more formal.

Ex.

▶ 王 先 生 ， 你 好 ！
Wáng xiānsheng,　　nǐ hǎo!
Hi, Mr. Wang!

▶ 陈 小 姐 ， 早 上 好 ！
Chén xiǎojiě,　　zǎoshàng hǎo!
Good morning, Miss Chen!

Time in Chinese:

	5 AM–12 PM	12–1 PM	1–6 PM	6 PM–12 AM	12–5 AM
	早上 zǎoshàng morning	中午 zhōngwǔ noon	下午 xiàwǔ afternoon	晚上 wǎnshàng evening	夜里 yèlǐ midnight

The following are greetings according to the time of day: morning, afternoon, and evening. The expressions are a little different between China and Taiwan. In Taiwan, greetings end with 安 (ān) instead of 好 (hǎo).

	good morning	good afternoon	good evening
China	早 上 好 zǎoshàng hǎo	下 午 好 xiàwǔ hǎo	晚 上 好 wǎnshàng hǎo
Taiwan	早安 zǎo'ān	午安 wǔ'ān	晚安 wǎn'ān

Part 2

好久①不②见③！ 好久不见！
Hǎo jiǔ bú jiàn! Hǎo jiǔ bú jiàn!
Long time no see! Long time no see!

你好吗④？ 我很好。
Nǐ hǎo ma? Wǒ hěn hǎo.
How are you? I'm great.

陈 先 生 他好吗？
Chén xiānsheng tā hǎo ma?
How is Mr. Chen?
他很好。
Tā hěn hǎo.
He's great.

最近⑥好吗？
Zuìjìn hǎo ma?
How have you been recently?
不错！
Búcuò!
Good!

Vocabulary

1 好久
hǎo jiǔ | *t.*
a very long time

2 不
bú | *adv.*
no; not

3 见
jiàn | *v.*
to see

4 吗
ma | *p.*
a question particle

5 很
hěn | *adv.*
very

6 最近
zuìjìn | *n.*
recently, lately

Language Notes

好久不见
hǎo jiǔ bú jiàn

To greet a friend we haven't seen for a long time, we can say 好久不见

Or

好久没见！
Hǎo jiǔ méi jiàn!

······ 好吗？
hǎo ma

By inserting a subject, such as a personal pronoun or proper noun, before 好吗, we can ask someone's condition.

Subject ＋ 好 吗？

▶ 你 好 吗？
Nǐ hǎo ma?
How are you?

Ex. ▶ 他 好 吗？
Tā hǎo ma?
How is he?

▶ 陈 先 生 好 吗？
Chén xiānsheng hǎo ma?
How is Mr. Chen?

By inserting a time word before 好吗, we can ask someone's condition within a certain time period.

Time Word ＋ 好 吗？

Ex. ▶ 最 近 好 吗？
Zuìjìn hǎo ma?
How have you been recently?

Extra Information

你好吗? is a common way to express our regards. We do not usually expect a long answer. In this situation, 我很好 can be used generally. If you want to describe your condition more specifically, here are some expressions:

很 好
hěn hǎo
great

不错
búcuò
good

还可以
hái kěyǐ
not bad

还行
hái xíng
fine

不太好
bú tài hǎo
not so good

Part 3

对不起。
Duìbùqǐ.
Sorry. / Excuse me.

没关系。
Méiguānxi.
It's OK.

请。
Qǐng.
Please.

谢谢！
Xièxie!
Thank you!

谢谢！
Xièxie!
Thank you!

不客气。
Bú kèqi.
You're welcome.

再见！
Zàijiàn!
Good-bye!

再见！
Zàijiàn!
Good-bye!

Language Notes

对不起 & 没关系 duìbùqǐ méiguānxi	To apologize, we can say 对不起.	**Or** 请原谅。 Qǐng yuánliàng. Please excuse me. 很抱歉。 Hěn bàoqiàn. I'm very sorry.
	To accept one's apology, we can say 没关系.	**Or** 没事儿。 Méishìr. It's nothing. 没什么。 Méishénme. It's nothing.

请 qǐng	When 请 appears alone, it expresses humbleness. We can also add verbs or verb phrases after 请 to make requests more polite.	**Ex.** ▶ 请 问 … Qǐngwèn… May I ask… ▶ 请 等 一 下 。 Qǐng děng yíxià. Please wait a moment.

谢谢 & 不客气 xièxie bú kèqi	To express our appreciation, we can say 谢谢.	**Or** 劳驾了。 Láojià le. Thank you. 麻烦您了。 Máfan nín le. Sorry to bother you.
	To accept one's gratitude, we can say 不客气.	**Or** 别 客气。 Bié kèqi. You're welcome. 不用谢。 Búyòng xiè. Don't mention it.

再见 zàijiàn	To say "good-bye" we use 再见 most often. We can also insert time words or places before 见 to mean "see you + time/place."	**Ex.** ▶ 明 天 见 ！ Míngtiān jiàn! See you tomorrow! ▶ 一 会 儿 见 ！ Yíhuìr jiàn! See you later! ▶ 北 京 见 ！ Běijīng jiàn! See you in Beijing!

Exercises

Choice

1. Please look at the following pictures. Assess each situation before filling in the appropriate response from the word bank.

Word Bank : a. 没关系。   b. 早上好!   c. 再见!   d. 谢谢!
          Méiguānxi.   Zǎoshàng hǎo!   Zàijiàn!   Xièxie!

2. Please read the following dialogue and choose the best answer.

(1) A：你好!
        Nǐ hǎo!

    B：_____   a. 你好吗?   b. 你好!   c. 我很好!   d. 谢谢!
                      Nǐ hǎo ma?   Nǐ hǎo!   Wǒ hěn hǎo!   Xièxie!

(2) A：最近好吗?
        Zuìjìn hǎo ma?

    B：_____   a. 谢谢!   b. 你好吗?   c. 不错!   d. 他很好。
                      Xièxie!   Nǐ hǎo ma?   Búcuò!   Tā hěn hǎo.

3. Plese read the following sentences and choose the best answer.

(1) It's the first day of school. While in the hall, your hat blows away. Mary, your classmate, walks by and picks it up for you.

① In order to show your appreciation, you would say:

a. 谢谢！
Xièxie!

b. 你好吗？
Nǐ hǎo ma?

c. 早上好！
Zǎoshàng hǎo!

d. 对不起！
Duìbùqǐ!

② Mary will respond to the above with:

a. 请。
Qǐng.

b. 不客气！
Bú kèqi!

c. 再见！
Zàijiàn!

d. 没关系。
Méiguānxi.

③ You haven't seen Mary since before your long summer vacation began. Of the four choices, choose the most suitable conversation.

a. Q: 陈先生好吗？
Chén xiānsheng hǎo ma?

A: 我很好。
Wǒ hěn hǎo.

b. Q: 最近好吗？
Zuìjìn hǎo ma?

A: 他很好。
Tā hěn hǎo.

c. Q: 好久不见！
Hǎo jiǔ bú jiàn!

A: 好久不见！
Hǎo jiǔ bú jiàn!

d. Q: 请！
Qǐng!

A: 谢谢！
Xièxie!

④ Your leg is suddenly hit by a baseball. A little boy runs up to you and says:

a. 对不起！
Duìbùqǐ!

b. 谢谢！
Xièxie!

c. 再见！
Zàijiàn!

d. 你好！
Nǐ hǎo!

⑤ Your leg hurts, but you want to forgive the boy, so you say:

a. 不用谢！
Búyòng xiè!

b. 别客气！
Bié kèqi!

c. 请等一下！
Qǐng děng yíxià!

d. 没关系。
Méiguānxi.

(2) You are a salesman. You have arrived at the office in the early morning because you have an important meeting with one of your customers, Mr. Chen.

① While waiting for the elevator to come, you meet your boss. What can you say to him?

a. 晚上好！
Wǎnshàng hǎo!

b. 对不起！
Duìbùqǐ!

c. 谢谢！
Xièxie!

d. 早上好！
Zǎoshàng hǎo!

② You and your boss are waiting together for the elevator. When the elevator arrives, what can you say to your boss?

a. 你好！
Nǐ hǎo!

b. 请！
Qǐng!

c. 没关系。
Méiguānxi.

d. 好久不见！
Hǎo jiǔ bú jiàn!

③ Now you are in the conference room. When Mr. Chen arrives, you shake his hand and say:

a. 陈先生，你好！
Chén xiānsheng, nǐ hǎo!

b. 很抱歉，陈先生。
Hěn bàoqiàn, Chén xiānsheng.

c. 别客气。
Bié kèqi.

d. 明天见。
Míngtiān jiàn.

④ If you want to ask how Mr. Chen has been, you say:

a. 你好！
Nǐ hǎo!

b. 下午好！
Xiàwǔ hǎo!

c. 最近好吗？
Zuìjìn hǎo ma?

d. 你很好吗？
Nǐ hěn hǎo ma?

⑤ Following the above, Mr. Chen can respond:

a. 你好！
Nǐ hǎo!

b. 晚上好！
Wǎnshàng hǎo!

c. 不错！
Búcuò!

d. 你好吗？
Nǐ hǎo ma?

Sitcom 轻喜剧

A Chance Encounter I

In this lesson, we will practice greeting other people. We will also learn how to introduce ourselves and how to ask and answer questions related to nationality.

Sentence Focus

Part 1   请问你叫什么名字？

Part 2   我姓金，叫明俊。   我是王文正。

Part 3   你是日本人吗？   你是哪国人？

林莉莉

Lín   Lìli

- 21 years old
- Sweet and easygoing
- Enjoys singing and cooking

王文正

Wáng Wénzhèng

- 21 years old
- Energetic and smart
- Enjoys sports and movies

金明俊

Jīn   Míngjùn

- 22 years old
- An exchange student at Live University
- Interested in studying Chinese and learning about culture

Part 1

CDR1-U4-P1

Suddenly, it begins to rain hard. Wenzheng is hiding from the rain under a pavilion, and Lily runs in to join him. She runs into Wenzheng.

莉莉:
Lìli

对不起！对不起！
Duìbùqǐ! Duìbùqǐ!

Lily: I'm sorry! I'm sorry!

文正:
Wénzhèng

没关系。没关系。
Méiguānxi. Méiguānxi.

Wenzheng: It's OK. It's OK.

莉莉:

真的很抱歉！
Zhēnde hěn bàoqiàn!

I'm really sorry!

文正:

没关系。
Méiguānxi.

It's OK.

你好！我叫①王文正。请问②你叫什么③名字④？
Nǐ hǎo! Wǒ jiào Wáng Wénzhèng. Qǐngwèn nǐ jiào shénme míngzi?

Hi! My name is Wenzheng Wang. May I ask what your name is?

莉莉:

你好，我叫林莉莉。
Nǐ hǎo, wǒ jiào Lín Lìli.

Hi! My name is Lily Lin.

Wenzheng sees that Lily's clothes are wet and wants to give her some tissue, but he isn't careful and drops his books on Lily's feet.

文正:

对不起！对不起！
Duìbùqǐ! Duìbùqǐ!

I'm sorry! I'm sorry!

Vocabulary

❶ 叫 | *v.*
jiào | to call, to be called

❷ 请问 | *ce.*
qǐngwèn | May I ask . . .

❸ 什么 | *qw.*
shéme | what

❹ 名字 | *n.*
míngzi | name

Language Notes

真的
zhēnde

As an adverb, 真的 means "really" or "indeed." We often use 真的 before 很 for emphasis.

▶ 真的很抱歉!
Zhēnde hěn bàoqiàn!
I'm really sorry!

▶ 真的很好!
Zhēnde hěn hǎo!
It's really good!

You can also use 真的 in exclamatory or interrogative sentences.

A: 我拿到奖学金了!
Wǒ nádào jiǎngxuéjīn le!
I got the scholarship!

B: 真的吗? (exclamatory)
Zhēnde ma?
Really?

A: 我很好。
Wǒ hěn hǎo.
I'm good.

B: 真的吗? (interrogative)
Zhēnde ma?
Really?

叫
jiào

叫 means "to call" or "to be called." We usually use 叫 to give our name, whether it is our full name or just our first name.

你叫什么名字?
Nǐ jiào shénme míngzi?
What's your name?

我叫林莉莉。
Wǒ jiào Lín Lìli.
My name is Lily Lin.

Q

A

他叫什么名字?
Tā jiào shénme míngzi?
What's his name?

他叫文正。
Tā jiào Wénzhèng.
His name is Wenzheng.

31

Part 2

CDR1-U4-P2

Mingjun, another student at Live University, happens to see the accident. He hands Lily a tissue.

莉莉:
Lìli

谢谢！
Xièxie!

Lily: Thank you!

明俊:
Míngjùn

不客气！
Bú kèqi!

Mingjun: You are welcome!

你好， 我姓①金， 叫明俊。
Nǐ hǎo, Wǒ xìng Jīn jiào Míngjùn.

Hello, my last name is Kim, and my first name is Mingjun.

请问你叫什么名字？
Qǐngwèn nǐ jiào shéme míngzi?

My I ask what your name is?

莉莉:

你好！我叫林莉莉。
Nǐ hǎo! Wǒ jiào Lín Lìli.

Hi! My name is Lily Lin.

文正:
Wénzhèng

我是②王文正。 你好！
Wǒ shì Wáng Wénzhèng. Nǐ hǎo!

Wenzheng: Hi! I am Wenzheng Wang.

明俊:

你好！
Nǐ hǎo!

Mingjun: Hello!

Vocabulary

❶ 姓
xìng | *n. / v.*
last name; to be surnamed

❷ 是
shì | *v.*
am/are/is

Language Notes

姓······, 叫······
xìng   jiào

"姓…, 叫…" is a more formal way to introduce ourselves. We can use this sentence pattern to give our first name or our last name. 姓 means "family name." It can be used as a noun or a verb.

▶ 我 姓 林 ， 叫 莉 莉 。
Wǒ xìng Lín,   jiào   Lìli.
My last name is Lin, and my first name is Lily.

▶ 他 姓 金 ， 叫 明 俊 。
Tā xìng Jīn,   jiào Míngjùn.
His last name is Kim, and his first name is Mingjun.

是
shì

是 means "to be (am, are, is, were, etc.)." It can be used to connect two nouns or pronouns that are in some way equivalent.

▶ 我 是 王 文 正 。
Wǒ shì Wáng Wénzhèng.
I am Wenzheng Wang.

▶ 我 是 中 国 人 。
Wǒ shì Zhōngguó rén.
I am Chinese.

▶ 王 文 正 是 中 国 人 。
Wáng Wénzhèng shì Zhōngguó rén.
Wenzheng Wang is Chinese.

Extra Information

When asking someone's name, we usually start with 请问 (qǐngwèn, May I ask . . .) to show courtesy. We can also use 贵姓 (guìxìng, your honorable surname) to find out someone's last name. This is a very formal expression. To respond to the question politely, we use 敝姓 (bìxìng, my humble surname) to introduce our own last name. The following are examples of more formal Chinese introductions:

Q 请 问 您 贵 姓 ？
Qǐngwèn nín guìxìng?
May I ask what your last name is?

A 敝 姓 王 ， 请 叫 我 文 正 。
Bìxìng Wáng,   qǐng jiào wǒ Wénzhèng.
My last name is Wang. Please call me Wenzheng.

Part 3

CDR1-U4-P3

Lily notices that Mingjun is holding a copy of *Live Interactive Chinese*.

莉莉：
Lìli

明俊，你是日本人①吗？
Míngjùn, nǐ shì Rìběn rén ma?

Lily: Are you Japanese, Mingjun?

明俊：
Míngjùn

不，我不是日本人。
Bù, wǒ bú shì Rìběn rén.

Mingjun: No, I'm not Japanese.

文正：
Wénzhèng

你是哪国人②？
Nǐ shì nǎ guó rén?

Wenzheng: What's your nationality?

明俊：

我是韩国人③。
Wǒ shì Hánguó rén.

I'm Korean.

The class bell rings. Lily looks at her watch and needs to hurry off to class.

莉莉：

再见！
Zàijiàn!

Good-bye!

明俊：

再见！
Zàijiàn!

Good-bye!

文正：

再见！
Zàijiàn!

Bye!

Vocabulary

❶ 日本 | n. Japan
Rìběn

日本人 | n. Japanese
Rìběn rén

❷ 哪 | qw. which
nǎ

哪国人 | n. which nationality
nǎ guó rén

❸ 韩国 | n. Korea
Hánguó

韩国人 | n. Korean
Hánguó rén

日本人　韩国人

Language Notes

吗
ma

吗 is added to the end of a declarative statement and is used to form a question. To respond to this type of question, we have to give a positive or negative answer. For example, to the question "是…吗?" we answer 是 (shì) for a positive answer and 不是 (bú shì) for a negative answer.

Statement ＋ 吗?

Q 他是文正吗？
Tā shì Wénzhèng ma?

Is he Wenzheng?

A 是，他是文正。
Shì,　tā shì Wénzhèng.

Yes, he is Wenzheng.

Or 不是，他不是文正。
Bú shì,　tā bú shì Wénzhèng.

No, he is not Wenzheng.

哪
nǎ

哪 is an interrogative particle. The phrase 哪国人 is used to ask someone's nationality.

Q 你是哪国人？
Nǐ shì nǎ guó rén?

What's your nationality?

A 我是韩国人。
Wǒ shì Hánguó rén.

I am Korean.

Or 我是中国人。
Wǒ shì Zhōngguó rén.

I am Chinese.

Me

CDR1 - U5 - P1

Hi! Hi! Hi! Hi!

我是 由纪　我是 汤姆
Wǒ shì　Yóujì.　Wǒ shì Tāngmǔ.
I'm Yuki. I'm Tom.

Hello! Hello! Hello! Hello!

我来自❶日本　我来自美国
Wǒ lái zì　Rìběn.　Wǒ lái zì Měiguó.
I'm from Japan. I'm from the United States.

Hi! Hi! Hi! Hi!

我叫 由纪　我叫 汤姆
Wǒ jiào　Yóujì.　Wǒ jiào Tāngmǔ.
I'm Yuki. I'm Tom.

Hello! Hello! Hello! Hello!

我很可爱❷我很帅❸
Wǒ hěn kě'ài.　Wǒ hěn shuài.
I'm very cute. I'm very handsome.

Hi! Hi! Hi! Hi! Hi! Hi!

Vocabulary

你问我是谁
Nǐ wèn wǒ shì shéi?
You asked who I am?

我再^❹说^❺一次^❻
Wǒ zài shuō yí cì.
Let me tell you one more time.

Hi! Hi! Hi! Hi! Hi! Hi!

我是由纪 我是汤姆
Wǒ shì Yóujì. Wǒ shì Tāngmǔ.
I'm Yuki. I'm Tom.

Hi! Hi! Hi! Hi! Hi! Hi!

你问我是谁 我再说一次
Nǐ wèn wǒ shì shéi? Wǒ zài shuō yí cì.
You asked who I am? Let me tell you one more time.

Hi! Hi! Hi! Hi! Hi! Hi!

我是由纪 我是汤姆
Wǒ shì Yóujì. Wǒ shì Tāngmǔ.
I'm Yuki. I'm Tom.

❶ 来自 | v.
lái zì | to come from

❷ 可爱 | sv.
kě'ài | to be cute; to be adorable

❸ 帅 | sv.
shuài | to be handsome

❹ 再 | adv.
zài | again

❺ 说 | v.
shuō | to say

❻ 次 | m.
cì | time

Sayonara Good-bye

再见 再见
zàijiàn! zàijiàn!
Good-bye! Good-bye!

See you next time.

Exercises

Listening

Look at the pictures below and listen to the recording. Choose the answer that best fits the question you hear.

a. 王小莉
Wáng Xiǎolì

b. 李 正
Lǐ Zhèng

c. 小林爱子
Xiǎolín Àizǐ

☐ (1) a. 是，王小莉是韩国人。
　　　 Shì, Wáng Xiǎolì shì Hánguó rén.

　　 b. 不是，王小莉不是中国人。
　　　 Bú shì, Wáng Xiǎolì bú shì Zhōngguó rén.

　　 c. 不是，王小莉不是韩国人。
　　　 Bú shì, Wáng Xiǎolì bú shì Hánguó rén.

☐ (2) a. 李 正 是 韩 国 人 。
　　　 Lǐ Zhèng shì Hánguó rén.

　　 b. 是，李 正 是 韩 国 人 。
　　　 Shì, Lǐ Zhèng shì Hánguó rén.

　　 c. 小 林 爱 子 是 韩 国 人 。
　　　 Xiǎolín Àizǐ shì Hánguó rén.

☐ (3) a. 王 小 莉 是 中 国 人 。
　　　 Wáng Xiǎolì shì Zhōngguó rén.

　　 b. 小 林 爱 子 是 日 本 人 。
　　　 Xiǎolín Àizǐ shì Rìběn rén.

　　 c. 李 正 是 日 本 人 。
　　　 Lǐ Zhèng shì Rìběn rén.

Choice

Choose the best answer to complete the dialogues.

☐ (4) 王小莉：李正，你好！
Wáng Xiǎolì:Lǐ Zhèng, nǐ hǎo!

李正：＿＿＿＿＿＿＿＿＿。
Lǐ Zhèng:

    a. 很好！   b. 你好！   c. 不好。
       Hěn hǎo!   Nǐ hǎo!   Bù hǎo.

☐ (5) 小林爱子：我叫小林爱子，你叫什么名字？
Xiǎolín Àizǐ: Wǒ jiào Xiǎolín Àizǐ, nǐ jiào shénme míngzi?

王小莉：＿＿＿＿＿＿＿＿＿。
Wáng Xiǎolì:

    a. 我姓小莉。   b. 我叫小莉。   c. 我叫王。
       Wǒ xìng Xiǎolì.   Wǒ jiào Xiǎolì.   Wǒ jiào Wáng.

☐ (6) 李正：我来自韩国，你呢？
Lǐ Zhèng: Wǒ lái zì Hánguó, nǐ ne?

小林爱子：＿＿＿＿＿＿＿＿＿。
Xiǎolín Àizi:

    a. 我不是日本人。   b. 是，我是日本人   c. 我是日本人。
       Wǒ bú shì Rìběn rén.   Shì, wǒ shì Rìběn rén.   Wǒ shì Rìběn rén.

☐ (7) 王小莉：我是中国人。你是中国人吗？
Wáng Xiǎolì: Wǒ shì Zhōngguó rén. Nǐ shì Zhōngguó rén ma?

李正：＿＿＿＿＿＿＿＿＿。
Lǐ Zhèng:

    a. 我不是韩国人。   b. 是，我是中国人。   c. 不是，我是韩国人。
       Wǒ bú shì Hánguó rén.   Shì, wǒ shì Zhōngguó rén.   Bú shì, wǒ shì Hánguó rén.

☐ (8) 小林爱子：最近好吗？
Xiǎolín Àizǐ: Zuìjìn hǎo ma?

李正：＿＿＿＿＿＿＿＿＿！
Lǐ Zhèng:

    a. 他很好！   b. 还不错！   c. 不客气。
       Tā hěn hǎo!   Hái búcuò!   Bú kèqi.

Asking for Directions I

Part 1

CDR1 - U6 - P1

Q

请问 ＿＿＿＿＿＿ 怎么走?

Qǐngwèn   zěnme zǒu?

Excuse me. How can I get to ＿＿＿＿＿＿?

Ex. 请问故宫博物院怎么走?

Qǐngwèn Gùgōng Bówùyuàn zěnme zǒu?

Excuse me. How can I get to the Palace Museum?

Or 在北京 In Beijing

请问王府井大街怎么走?

Qǐngwèn Wángfǔjǐng Dàjiē zěnme zǒu?

Excuse me. How can I get to Wangfujing Street?

请问长城怎么走?

Qǐngwèn Chángchéng zěnme zǒu?

Excuse me. How can I get to the Great Wall?

在台北 In Taipei

请问台北101怎么走?

Qǐngwèn Táiběi Yī Líng Yī zěnme zǒu?

Excuse me. How can I get to Taipei 101?

请问士林夜市怎么走?

Qǐngwèn Shìlín Yèshì zěnme zǒu?

Excuse me. How can I get to Shilin Night Market?

Extra Information

The Palace Museum in Beijing, also known as the Forbidden City, was once home to a long line of Chinese emperors. It is nearly 600 years old and has 800 buildings with some 8,000 rooms. Designated as a world heritage site in 1987 by UNESCO, the museum now serves as a tourist attraction.

Give It a Try

北京 Beijing

故宫博物院
Gùgōng Bówùyuàn

The Palace Museum

长 城
Chángchéng

The Great Wall

王府井大街
Wángfǔjǐng Dàjiē

Wangfujing Street

台北 Taipei

故宫博物院
Gùgōng Bówùyuàn

The National Palace Museum

台北101
Táiběi Yī Líng Yī

Taipei 101

士林夜市
Shìlín Yèshì

Shilin Night Market

Part 2

CDR1 - U6 - P2

A

你可以 ____ 到天安门西站。
Nǐ kěyǐ ____ dào Tiān'ānmén Xī Zhàn.
You can ____ to Tian'anmen West Station.

Ex. 你可以 乘 地铁 到 天安门西站。
Nǐ kěyǐ chéng dìtiě dào Tiān'ānmén Xī Zhàn.
You can take the subway to Tian'anmen West Station.

Or 在北京 In Beijing

你可以 乘 公交车 到 天安门 西站。
Nǐ kěyǐ chéng gōngjiāochē dào Tiān'ānmén Xī Zhàn.
You can take a bus to Tian'anmen West Station.

你可以 乘 出租车 到 天安门 西站。
Nǐ kěyǐ chéng chūzūchē dào Tiān'ānmén Xī Zhàn.
You can take a taxi to Tian'anmen West Station.

在台北 In Taipei

你可以搭火车到台北车站。
Nǐ kěyǐ dā huǒchē dào Táiběi Chēzhàn.
You can take a train to Taipei Main Station.

你可以骑摩托车到台北车站。
Nǐ kěyǐ qí mótuōchē dào Táiběi Chēzhàn.
You can ride a motorcycle to Taipei Main Station.

Extra Information

More Information Online
• The Palace Museum in Beijing http://www.dpm.org.cn/
• The National Palace Museum in Taipei http://www.npm.gov.tw/

Give It a Try

乘 地铁
chéng dìtiě
to take the subway

乘 火车
chéng huǒchē
to take a train

乘 公交车
chéng gōngjiāochē
to take a bus

乘 出租车
chéng chūzūchē
to take a taxi

骑 自行车
qí zìxíngchē
to ride a bicycle

骑 摩托车
qí mótuōchē
to ride a motorcycle

Different Usages: China and Taiwan

	China	Taiwan
to take the subway	乘 地铁 chéng dìtiě	搭捷运 (MRT) dā jiéyùn
to take a bus	乘 公交车、巴士 chéng gōngjiāochē、 bāshì	搭公车、巴士 dā gōngchē、 bāshì
to take a taxi	乘 出租车 chéng chūzūchē	搭计程车 dā jìchéngchē
to ride a bicycle	骑自行车 qí zìxíngchē	骑脚踏车 qí jiǎotàchē

Sentence Patterns 中文句型

Exercises

Matching

Match the pictures below with the corresponding vehicles.

(1) 公 交 车   (2) 地 铁   (3) 出 租 车   (4) 自 行 车   (5) 摩 托 车   (6) 火 车
gōngjiāochē   dìtiě   chūzūchē   zìxíngchē   mótuōchē   huǒchē

a.   b.   c.   d.   e.   f.

Choice

1. Please choose the correct order.

☐ (1) ① 请 问   ② 怎 么 走   ③ 长   城
        qǐngwèn   zěnme zǒu   Chángchéng

   a. ③②①   b. ①②③   c. ①③②

☐ (2) ① 你可以   ② 出 租 车   ③ 乘   ④ 到 长   城
        nǐ kěyǐ   chūzūchē   chéng   dào Chángchéng

   a. ④③②①   b. ①③②④   c. ①②③④

☐ (3) Q : ① 怎 么 走   ② 请 问   ③ 天 坛
          zěnme zǒu   qǐngwèn   Tiāntán
      A : ④ 巴 士   ⑤ 你可以   ⑥ 到 天 坛   ⑦ 搭
          bāshì   nǐ kěyǐ   dào Tiāntán   dā

   a. ②③① ⑤⑦④⑥   b. ③②① ④⑤⑥⑦   c. ①②③ ⑦⑥⑤④

2. Please complete the following dialogue based on the photos next to each question.

☐ (1) Q：请问紫禁城怎么走？
　　　　Qǐngwèn Zǐjìnchéng zěnme zǒu?

　　　A：＿＿＿＿＿＿＿＿＿＿＿＿。

　　　　a. 你可以搭公交车到紫禁城。　　　b. 你可以乘地铁到紫禁城。
　　　　　 Nǐ kěyǐ dā gōngjiāochē dào Zǐjìnchéng.　　　 Nǐ kěyǐ chéng dìtiě dào Zǐjìnchéng.

　　　　c. 你可以骑自行车到紫禁城。
　　　　　 Nǐ kěyǐ qí zìxíngchē dào Zǐjìnchéng.

☐ (2) Q：请问圆明园怎么走？
　　　　Qǐngwèn Yuánmíngyuán zěnme zǒu?

　　　A：＿＿＿＿＿＿＿＿＿＿＿＿。

　　　　a. 你可以搭公交车到圆明园。　　b. 你可以乘地铁到圆明园。
　　　　　 Nǐ kěyǐ dā gōngjiāochē dào Yuánmíngyuán.　　 Nǐ kěyǐ chéng dìtiě dào Yuánmíngyuán.

　　　　c. 你可以骑自行车到圆明园。
　　　　　 Nǐ kěyǐ qí zìxíngchē dào Yuánmíngyuán.

☐ (3) Q：请问台北１０１怎么走？
　　　　Qǐngwèn Táiběi Yī Líng Yī zěnme zǒu?

　　　A：＿＿＿＿＿＿＿＿＿＿＿＿。　　　or

　　　　a. 你可以乘出租车或公交车到台北车站。
　　　　　 Nǐ kěyǐ chéng chūzūchē huò gōngjiāochē dào Táiběi Chēzhàn.

　　　　b. 你可以骑自行车或摩托车到台北１０１。
　　　　　 Nǐ kěyǐ qí zìxíngchē huò mótuōchē dào Táiběi Yī Líng Yī.

　　　　c. 你可以乘出租车或公交车到台北１０１。
　　　　　 Nǐ kěyǐ chéng chūzūchē huò gōngjiāochē dào Táiběi Yī Líng Yī.

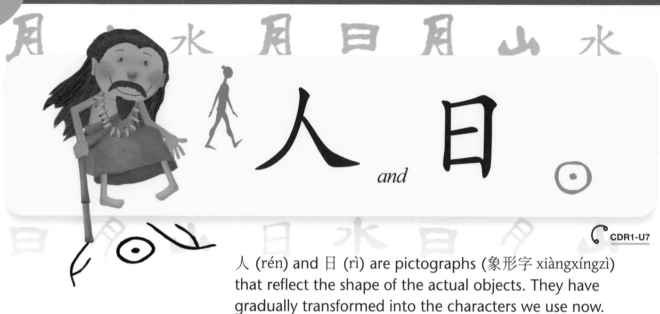

人 *and* 日

CDR1-U7

人 (rén) and 日 (rì) are pictographs (象形字 xiàngxíngzì) that reflect the shape of the actual objects. They have gradually transformed into the characters we use now.

Order

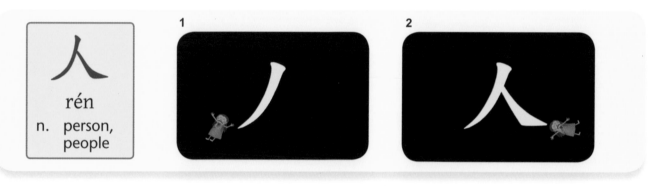

人
rén
n.   person, people

1

2

History

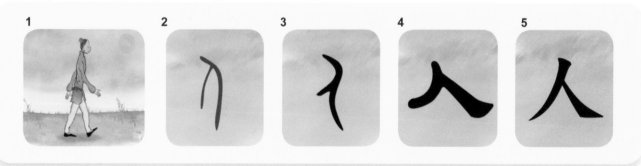

1   2   3   4   5

Examples

人	中国人	姚明是中国人。
rén	Zhōngguó rén	Yáo Míng shì Zhōngguó rén.
person, people	Chinese person / people	Yao Ming is Chinese.

Order

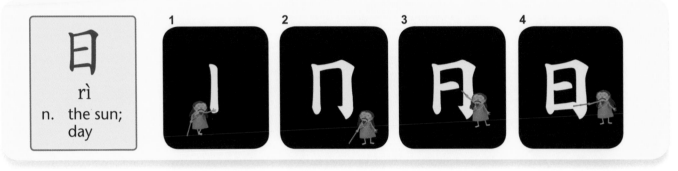

日
rì
n.   the sun;
     day

History

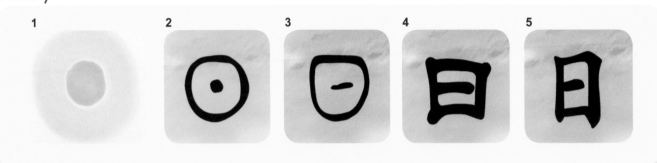

Examples

日
rì

the sun; day

星期日
Xīngqīrì

Sunday

今天是星期日。
Jīntiān shì Xīngqīrì.

Today is Sunday.

Give It a Try : Try to find "人" or "日" in the following pictures and circle them.

Chinese Noodles & Ordering

Part 1 Tableware

♪ CDR1 - U8 - P1

¹刀子
dāozi | n. knife

²叉子
chāzi | n. fork

³纸巾
zhǐjīn | n. napkin

⁴碗
wǎn | n. bowl

⁵杯子
bēizi | n. cup, glass

⁶盘子
pánzi | n. dish

⁷汤匙
tāngchí | n. spoon

⁸筷子
kuàizi | n. chopsticks

Part 2 Ordering

请问有 _____ 吗?
Qǐngwèn yǒu _____ ma?

Excuse me, do you have _____ ?

客人 : 请问有①炸酱面②吗?
Kèrén
Qǐngwèn yǒu zhájiàngmiàn ma?

Customer : Excuse me, do you have zhajiang noodles?

服务员 : 对不起, 我们没③有炸酱面。
Fúwùyuán
Duìbùqǐ, wǒmen méi yǒu zhájiàngmiàn.

Waiter/
Waitress : I'm sorry. We don't have zhajiang noodles.

客人 : 有牛肉面④吗?
Yǒu niúròumiàn ma?
Do you have beef noodle soup?

服务员 : 有。
Yǒu.
Yes, we do.

客人 : 我要⑤一碗⑥牛肉面。
Wǒ yào yì wǎn niúròumiàn.
I would like one bowl of beef noodle soup.

服务员 : 好, 请等⑦一下⑧。
Hǎo, qǐng děng yíxià.
No problem. Please wait a moment.

Vocabulary

① 有 | v.
yǒu | to have

② 炸酱面 | n.
zhájiàngmiàn | zhajiang noodles (noodles with meat sauce)

③ 没 | adv.
méi | no; not

④ 牛肉面 | n.
niúròumiàn | beef noodle soup

⑤ 要 | v.
yào | to want

⑥ 碗 | m.
wǎn | a bowl of

⑦ 等 | v.
děng | to wait

⑧ 一下 | nu.+m.
yíxià | a while

49

Part 3 Chinese-Style Noodles

炸酱面

In Beijing, people customarily have a bowl of Chinese zhajiang noodles on the summer solstice to usher in the hot weather. Whether they are having the noodles while sitting in a fancy five-star restaurant or squatting in the shade under the trees outside their own house, people tend to follow the same etiquette. They don't fret about being a gentleman or a lady, but gulp the noodles down and have another bowl. You can also invite your neighbors to join in since more people create more fun.

Many people prefer to make their own sauce. Relying on old family recipes and freshly rolled noodles, they are usually able to cook up something that tastes great.

A Closer Look at the Ingredients of Zhajiang Noodles

色拉油
sèlāyóu
oil

酱油
jiàngyóu
soy sauce

辣豆瓣酱
là dòubànjiàng
spicy bean sauce

糖
táng
sugar

肉馅
ròuxiàn
ground pork

小黄瓜
xiǎohuángguā
cucumber

大蒜
dàsuàn
garlic

面条
miàntiáo
noodles

牛肉面

Beef noodle soup is usually considered a traditional dish, but some variations have been recently added, including a health-oriented tomato and exotic curry. There's also a traditional "Sichuan beef noodle soup," which still tops every food lover's list. Sichuan (四川 Sìchuān), a province in southern China, is not credited with inventing beef noodle soup but rather for coming up with the seasoning recipe. By adding a Sichuan-style spicy bean sauce, cooks discovered something magical happened to the taste of the soup. It is the soup, which is much stronger than it used to be, that is the real reason the dish has become popular again.

A Closer Look at the Ingredients of Beef Noodle Soup

牛肉
niúròu
beef

大蒜
dàsuàn
garlic

姜
jiāng
ginger

青葱
qīngcōng
green onions

调料 包
tiáoliào bāo
spice bag

西红柿
xīhóngshì
tomato

酸菜
suāncài
pickled Chinese cabbage

面 条
miàntiáo
noodles

Exercises

Choice

1. Please fill in the box with the corresponding letter from the word bank.

Word Bank : a. 刀子   b. 叉子   c. 盘子   d. 杯子   e. 碗   f. 汤匙   g. 纸巾   h. 筷子
dāozi   chāzi   pánzi   bēizi   wǎn   tāngchí   zhǐjīn   kuàizi

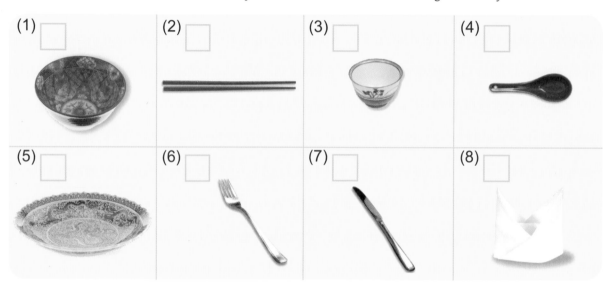

(1) ☐   (2) ☐   (3) ☐   (4) ☐

(5) ☐   (6) ☐   (7) ☐   (8) ☐

2. Please choose the word order that creates a correct sentence.

☐ (1) ①有   ②请问   ③炒面   ④吗
yǒu   qǐngwèn   chǎomiàn   ma

a. ③④②①   b. ②①③④   c. ④③②①

☐ (2) ①没有   ②对不起   ③我们   ④炒面
méiyǒu   duìbùqǐ   wǒmen   chǎomiàn

a. ②③①④   b. ①②③④   c. ②③④①

☐ (3) ①有   ②炒饭   ③吗   ④请问
yǒu   chǎofàn   ma   qǐngwèn

a. ①②③④   b. ③①④②   c. ④①②③

☐ (4) ①有   ②炒饭   ③我们   ④有
yǒu   chǎofàn   wǒmen   yǒu

a. ①③④②   b. ④①②③   c. ①②③④

3. Please fill in the blank with the corresponding letter to complete the conversation.

a. 请 问 有 牛 肉 面 吗	b. 谢 谢	c. 那 炸 酱 面 呢
Qǐngwèn yǒu niúròumiàn ma	Xièxie	Nà zhájiàngmiàn ne
d. 你 好	e. 我 要 一 碗 炸 酱 面	f. 我 还 要 一 杯 茶
Nǐ hǎo	Wǒ yào yì wǎn zhájiàngmiàn	Wǒ hái yào yì bēi chá

服务员： 你好！
Fúwùyuán: Nǐ hǎo!

客人： _____ 。_____ ?
kèrén:

服务员： 对不起， 我们没有牛肉面。
Fúwùyuán: Duìbùqǐ, wǒmen méiyǒu niúròumiàn.

客人： _____ ?
kèrén:

服务员： 有。
Fúwùyuán: Yǒu.

客人： _____ 。
kèrén:

服务员： 好，请等一下。
Fúwùyuán: Hǎo, qǐng děng yíxià.

客人： _____ 。
kèrén:

服务员： 好。
Fúwùyuán: hǎo.

客人： _____ !
kèrén:

53

Chinese Names & Beijing Dialect

Part 1 Chinese Names

Chinese names are divided into two parts, last names (姓, xìng) and first names (名, míng). Contrary to Western names, the 姓 always precedes the 名. In China, children usually take their father's last name. Sometimes, wives also place their husband's last names before their own. This custom is becoming less common.

Chinese family names also stand for a family's origin and pedigree. In former times, families with the same last name were not allowed to marry. This is no longer enforced.

Most Chinese family names are monosyllabic, such as 王 (Wáng), 林 (Lín), or 刘 (Liú). There are still a few disyllabic family names, such as 司马 (Sīmǎ) or 欧阳 (Ōuyáng). Parents usually give their children a beautiful and meaningful name. For example, if a child is named 明 (Míng), his parents probably hope for him or her to be "smart and bright."

Part 2 Beijing Dialect

Visitors to Beijing cannot help but notice the distinctive Beijing dialect, which has an obvious rolling pronunciation. In most of China, for instance, people say 花 (huā, flower). In Beijing, however, it becomes 花儿 (huār). You'll also hear 唱歌儿 (chànggēr, to sing) and 画画儿 (huàhuàr, to draw) in Beijing instead of 唱歌 (chànggē) and 画画 (huàhuà). 今儿个儿 (jīnrgr) means today, for which most people in China say 今天 (jīntiān, today).

There is also a lot of local slang. For "chat," for example, locals say 侃大山 (kǎndàshān). 侃 (kǎn) means "to boast." Young road-side female venders are called 大姐 (dàjiě, literally meaning "elder sister"), and 抠门儿(kōuménr) is said to describe a person who is very cheap. Taking a taxi is called 打的 (dǎdī). Taxi drivers are called 的哥 (dīgē, male taxi driver), 的姐 (dījiě, female taxi driver), or simply 师傅 (shīfù).

On your next trip to Beijing, see if you can pick up some new slang.

姓 last name	名 first name
xìng	míng
王 Wáng	小莉 Xiǎolì
欧阳 Ōuyáng	明 Míng

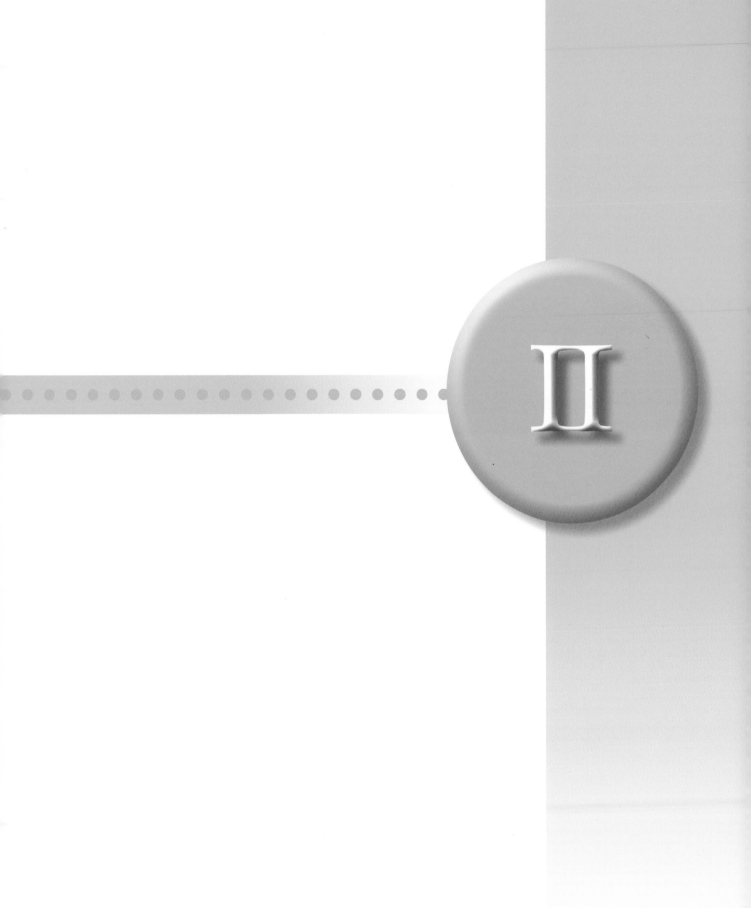

Easily Confused Sounds

Part 1

CDR2 - U1 - P1

In this lesson, we will compare some sounds that can be confusing to learners.

❶ Unaspirated and Aspirated Sounds: b/p, d/t, g/k

When pronouncing a sound that is not aspirated, such as b, d, g, the tissue remains still. While pronouncing an aspirated sound, such as p, t, k, the tissue vibrates lightly. Here are some exercises:

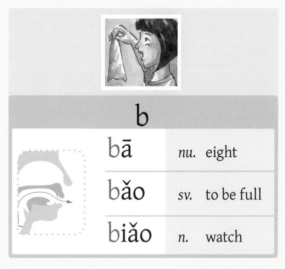

b		
bā	*nu.*	eight
bǎo	*sv.*	to be full
biǎo	*n.*	watch

p		
pā	*v.*	to lie prone
pǎo	*v.*	to run
piào	*n.*	ticket

d		
dà	*sv.*	to be big; to be large
diǎn	*n.*	dot; point

t		
tà	*v.*	to step on
tiǎn	*v.*	to lick

g		
gǒu	*n.*	dog
guà	*v.*	to hang on

k		
kǒu	*n.*	mouth
kuà	*v.*	to stride

Give it a Try

Listen to the recording and try to pronounce these sounds. Aspirated sounds are on the right side and unaspirated sounds are on the left side. You can put your palm in front of your mouth when you pronounce these sounds to check for aspiration.

b	p
bāo	pāo
bó	pó
bǐ	pǐ
bà	pà
d	**t**
dōu	tōu
dí	tí
dǎn	tǎn
dào	tào
g	**k**
guī	kuī
gé	ké
gǎn	kǎn
guài	kuài

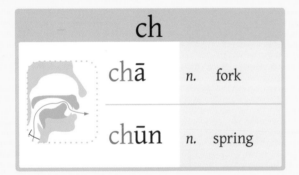

❷ Retroflex and Non-Retroflex Sounds: zh/z, ch/c, sh/s

The pronunciation of these three pairs is very similar. The only difference is in whether you turn up your tongue or not. To pronounce a retroflex sound, such as zh, ch, sh, turn up the tip of your tongue against the hard palate. To pronounce non-retroflex sounds, such as z, c, s, do not turn up your tongue, but place the tip of your tongue against the back of your teeth. Try the following exercises:

zh		
zhǎo	v.	to look for
Zhāng	n.	a Chinese family name

z		
zǎo	n.	morning
zāng	sv.	to be dirty

ch		
chā	n.	fork
chūn	n.	spring

c		
cā	v.	to wipe; to scrub
cūn	n.	village

sh		
shān	n.	mountain
shuì	v.	to sleep

s		
sān	nu.	three
suì	m.	a year (of age)

❸ Palatal and Blade Alveolar (Non-Retroflex) Sounds: j/z, q/c, x/s

To pronounce palatal sounds, such as j, q, x, raise the front of your tongue toward the hard palate to obstruct the breath, and then squeeze air out. To pronounce blade alveolar sounds, such as z, c, s, place the tip of your tongue against the back of your teeth and squeeze air out from between your teeth and tongue. Try the following examples:

j		
jù	*n.*	sentence
jiè	*v.*	to borrow

z		
zū	*v.*	to rent
zài	*adv.*	again

q		
qī	*nu.*	seven
qián	*n.*	money

c		
cì	*m.*	time(s)
cài	*n.*	dish

x		
xián	*sv.*	to be salty
xué	*v.*	to learn

s		
sǎn	*n.*	umbrella
suān	*sv.*	to be sour

Chinese Pronunciation 中文发音

unit 1

❹ Palatal and Blade Palatal (Retroflex) Sounds: j/zh, q/ch, x/sh

For beginners, it's not easy to differentiate the group of palatal sounds and blade alveolar sounds, as well as the group of palatal sounds and blade palatal sounds. The difference between a palatal and blade palatal sound is in how the tongue obstructs the breath. To pronounce palatal sounds, such as j, q, x, raise the front of your tongue toward the hard palate and let the air out. For blade palatal sounds, such as zh, ch, sh, however, turn up your tongue against the hard palate and let the air out. Try the following examples:

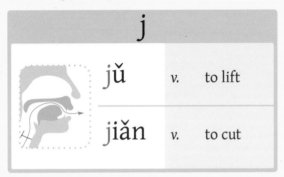

j		
jǔ	v.	to lift
jiǎn	v.	to cut

zh		
zhǔ	v.	to cook
zhàn	v.	to stand

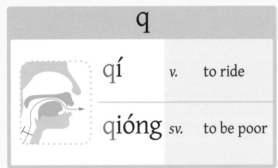

q		
qí	v.	to ride
qióng	sv.	to be poor

ch		
chí	sv.	to be late
chóng	n.	worm

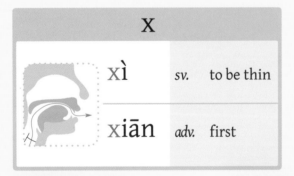
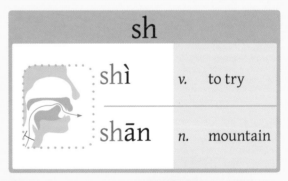

x		
xì	sv.	to be thin
xiān	adv.	first

sh		
shì	v.	to try
shān	n.	mountain

60

Part 2

❶ Front Nasal Finals and Back Nasal Finals: an/ang, en/eng

Learners often confuse the nasal final an with ang. Both sounds start with the a sound but end with different sounds. an ends with n while ang uses the back part of the nasal cavity to produce the ng sound. en and eng work in the same way. Both start with the e sound. But, once again, the endings are different.

an		
a wán	*v.*	to play
n chuán	*n.*	boat

ang		
a Wáng	*n.*	a Chinese family name
ng chuáng	*n.*	bed

en		
e mén	*n.*	door
n shēntǐ	*n.*	body

eng		
e dēng	*n.*	lamp; light
ng shēngrì	*n.*	birthday

61

❷ Simple Finals (Medials): u/ü

u and ü are two other sounds that often confuse learners. They are both pronounced with rounded lips. The key to pronouncing them correctly is the position of your tongue. When pronouncing u, round your lips and use a high back tongue blade. To get ü correct, also round your lips and use a high front tongue blade.

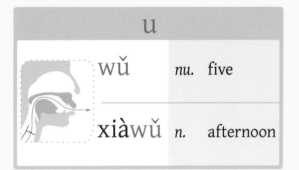

u			
wǔ	*nu.*	five	
xiàwǔ	*n.*	afternoon	

ü			
yuǎn	*sv.*	to be far	
xiàyǔ	*v.*	to rain	

❸ Other Sounds: f/h, n/l, r/l, uo/ou

f and h sounds rely on different air friction. The f sound is pronounced with the upper teeth touching the lower lip while the h sound is produced by letting air out between the tongue and soft palate.

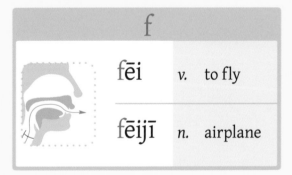

f			
fēi	*v.*	to fly	
fēijī	*n.*	airplane	

h			
hēi	*n/sv.*	black; to be dark	
háizi	*n.*	child	

You need the tip of the tongue to pronounce both n and l. But the position of the tip of tongue is different. For n, touch the upper ridge of the teeth. For l, hold the tip back further than for n.

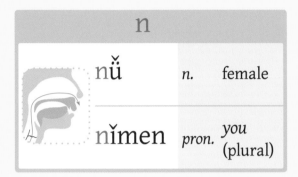

n			
nǚ	*n.*	female	
nǐmen	*pron.*	you (plural)	

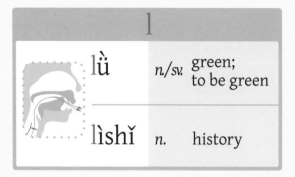

l			
lǜ	*n./sv.*	green; to be green	
lìshǐ	*n.*	history	

When pronouncing r, retroflex the tip of your tongue to the hard palate to obstruct the air. For l, touch the tip of your tongue to the back of the upper ridge of the teeth. Let air out from both sides of the tongue.

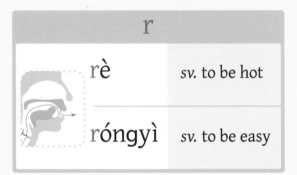

r		
rè	*sv.*	to be hot
róngyì	*sv.*	to be easy

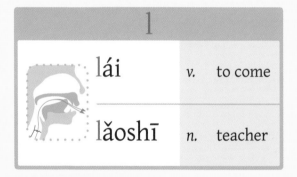

l		
lái	*v.*	to come
lǎoshī	*n.*	teacher

uo and ou are both compound vowels, so special attention should be paid to the shape of the lips when you start and finish pronouncing them. When pronouncing uo, start from u and finish with o. For ou, start from o and finish with u.

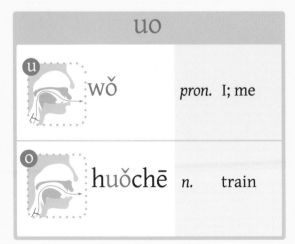

uo		
wǒ	*pron.*	I; me
huǒchē	*n.*	train

ou		
gǒu	*n.*	dog
yóuyǒng	*v.*	to swim

Chinese Pronunciation 中文发音

Exercises

Listening

1. Listen to the recording, and circle the word with the correct initial.

Ex. 〔j〕 寄 纸

(1) 〔t〕 灯   疼   (2) 〔zh〕 早   找

(3) 〔s〕 西   四   (4) 〔b〕 冰   瓶

(5) 〔c〕 擦   茶

2. Listen to the recording. Repeat and then circle the correct initial.

Ex. 〔g〕 〔q〕

(1) 〔g〕〔k〕   (2) 〔s〕〔sh〕   (3) 〔q〕〔c〕   (4) 〔x〕〔sh〕

3. Listen to the recording and then write down the initials you hear.

Ex. __b__ ā __p__ ā

(1) ____ ù ____ ù   (2) ____ uān ____ uān

(3) ____ ào ____ ào   (4) ____ iàn ____ àn

4. Listen to the recording and write the pinyin you hear. (There is no need to write tone marks for this exercise.)

 chu a n

(1) w_____

(2) m____ r____

(3) l_____ qiu

(4) n____ h____

(5) t____ f____

5. Listen to the recording and check the box that contains the sound for each question.

 an   ☑A   ☐B   ☑C   ☐D

(1) ü   ☐A   ☐B   ☐C   ☐D

(2) l   ☐A   ☐B   ☐C   ☐D

(3) en   ☐A   ☐B   ☐C   ☐D

(4) h   ☐A   ☐B   ☐C   ☐D

6. Listen to the recording and choose the correct pinyin.

 máng   A   B   Ⓒ   D

(1) tōu   A   B   C   D

(2) hù   A   B   C   D

(3) huán   A   B   C   D

(4) xǐyàn   A   B   C   D

Family Members

Do you know how to refer to family members in Chinese?

CDR2-U2

爷爷
yéye | *n.* paternal grandfather

奶奶
nǎinai | *n.* paternal grandmother

爸爸
bàba | *n.* father

妈妈
māma | *n.* mother

外公 / 姥爷
wàigōng　lǎoyé | *n.* maternal grandfather

外婆 / 姥姥
wàipó　lǎolao | *n.* maternal grandmother

哥哥
gēge | *n.*
elder bother

弟弟
dìdi | *n.*
younger brother

我 | *n.*
wǒ | me

姐姐
jiějie | *n.*
elder sister

妹妹
mèimei | *n.*
younger sister

Chinese people put great emphasis on family. There are, for this reason, many ways to address family members.

- For grandfather, we say 祖父 (zǔfù) while grandmother is 祖母 (zǔmǔ). 祖父母(zǔfù-mǔ) means grandparents. Similarly, we can call our maternal grandfather 外祖父 (wàizǔfù), while our maternal grandmother is 外祖母 (wàizǔmǔ). Together, they are 外祖父母 (wàizǔfù-mǔ).

- When parents introduce their children to other people, they often call their sons 儿子 (érzi) and daughters 女儿 (nǚér).

- "Siblings" in Chinese is 兄弟姐妹 (xiōng-dì-jiě-mèi).

Picture Dictionary 图解词典

Exercises

Matching

1. Please look at the picture, and then read the sentences on the left. Then, match the sentences with the correct Chinese vocabulary words.

Hi, I'm Julia. There are seven people in my family. I have one younger brother and one younger sister. This is a picture of my family. Now, I want to introduce my family to you.

Julia

(1) The person behind me is my younger brother.

(2) The person in the middle is my grandfather.

(3) The person behind my grandfather is my mom.

(4) The person in front of me is my younger sister.

(5) The person on my mother's left is my father.

(6) The person on my grandfather's left is my grandmother.

a. 爷爷
yéye

b. 奶奶
nǎinai

c. 爸爸
bàba

d. 妈妈
māma

e. 哥哥
gēge

f. 姐姐
jiějie

g. 弟弟
dìdi

h. 妹妹
mèimei

2. Please look at the following picture. Label each family member with the correct corresponding letter.

Word Bank: a. 妹妹   b. 爸爸   c. 妈妈   d. 哥哥
　　　　　　 mèimei   bàba   māma   gēge

(2) ☐   (3) ☐

(1) ☐

(4) ☐

Word Bank: a.爸爸   b.妈妈   c.姐姐   d.弟弟   e.爷爷   f.奶奶
　　　　　　 bàba   māma   jiějie   dìdi   yéye   nǎinai

(5) ☐   (10) ☐

(6) ☐

(9) ☐

(7) ☐   (8) ☐

Introducing Family Members

Part 1

CDR2-U3-P1

Q 你有兄弟姐妹[1]吗?
Nǐ yǒu xiōng-dì-jiě-mèi ma?
Do you have any siblings?

A 有。
Yǒu.
Yes, I do.

Q 你有几[2]个[3]兄弟姐妹?
Nǐ yǒu jǐ ge xiōng-dì-jiě-mèi?
How many siblings do you have?

A 我有一[4]个姐姐, 两[5]个弟弟。
Wǒ yǒu yí ge jiějie, liǎng ge dìdi.
I have an elder sister and two younger brothers.

Q 你家[6]有几口[7]人?
Nǐ jiā yǒu jǐ kǒu rén?
How many people are there in your family?

A 我家有六[8]口人。
Wǒ jiā yǒu liù kǒu rén.
There are six people in my family.

Q 你家有什么人?
Nǐ jiā yǒu shénme rén?
Who are the members of your family?

A 我家有爸爸、妈妈、姐姐、两个
Wǒ jiā yǒu bàba、 māma、 jiějie、 liǎng ge
弟弟和[9]我。 They are my father, mother, elder sister,
dìdi hé wǒ. two younger brothers, and me.

Vocabulary

❶ 兄弟姐妹
xiōng-dì-jiě-mèi
n. brothers and sisters; siblings

❷ 几
jǐ
qw. how many

❸ 个
ge
m. a common measure word for people and items

❹ 一
yī
nu. one

❺ 两
liǎng
nu. two (only used with measure words)

❻ 家
jiā
n. home; family

❼ 口
kǒu
m. a measure word for people

❽ 六
liù
nu. six

❾ 和
hé
conj. and

Language Notes

有 …… 吗？
yǒu   ma

有 means "to have" or "to possess." Adding 吗 at the end of a 有 sentence makes it an interrogative, which is used to confirm whether someone has something or not. To respond to the "有…吗" question, we can simply say 有 for an affirmative answer or 没有 for a negative answer.

Q
你有哥哥吗？
Nǐ yǒu gēge ma?
Do you have elder brothers?

你有书吗？
Nǐ yǒu shū ma?
Do you have books?

A
我没有哥哥，我有姐姐。
Wǒ méiyǒu gēge, wǒ yǒu jiějie.
I don't have elder brothers. I have an elder sister.

我没有书。
Wǒ méiyǒu shū.
I don't have books.

…… 什么人？
shénme rén

什么 is a question word. We insert a noun after 什么 to ask for further details. For example, 什么 plus 人 is used to ask about one's identity.

Q
你家有什么人？
Nǐ jiā yǒu shénme rén?
Who are the members of your family?

他是什么人？
Tā shì shénme rén?
Who is he?

A
我家有爸爸、妈妈和我。
Wǒ jiā yǒu bàba māma hé wǒ.
The members of my family are my father, mother, and me.

他是我哥哥。
Tā shì wǒ gēge.
He is my elder brother.

Extra Information

兄弟姐妹
xiōng-dì-jiě-mèi

兄弟姐妹 means "siblings." 兄 means "elder brother." 弟 means "younger brother." 姐 means "elder sister." 妹 means "younger sister." When a family has only one child, we call him 独生子 (dúshēngzǐ, the only son), or her 独生女 (dúshēngnǚ, the only daughter).

Part 2

Q 这是你弟弟吗？
Zhè shì nǐ dìdi ma?
Is this your younger brother?

A 不是，这是我哥哥。
Bú shì, zhè shì wǒ gēge.
No, this is my elder brother.

Q 她是你妹妹吗？
Tā shì nǐ mèimei ma?
Is she your younger sister?

A 是，她是我妹妹。
Shì, tā shì wǒ mèimei.
Yes, she is my younger sister.

Q 这是谁？
Zhè shì shéi?
Who is this?

A 这是我姐姐。
Zhè shì wǒ jiějie.
This is my elder sister.

Q 他是谁？
Tā shì shéi?
Who is he?

A 他是我弟弟。
Tā shì wǒ dìdi.
He is my younger brother.

Language Notes

是 ...... 吗 ?
shì   ma

是 is used to connect two nouns or pronouns that are in some way equivalent. By inserting 吗 at the end of a sentence, we can form a question. We often use this kind of question to reconfirm the information we want to know.

Q

这是他妹妹吗？
Zhè shì tā mèimei ma?
Is this his younger sister?

他是你哥哥吗？
Tā shì nǐ gēge ma?
Is he your elder brother?

A

不是，这不是他妹妹。
Bú shì, zhè bú shì tā mèimei.
No, this is not his younger sister.

不是，他是我弟弟。
Bú shì, tā shì wǒ dìdi.
No, he is my younger brother.

谁
shéi

We use 谁 to ask about people we do not know. To respond to this type of question, we usually include information such as the person's identity, nationality, profession, or their relationship to the speaker or another person.

...... 是 谁 ?

Q

这是谁？
Zhè shì shéi?
Who is this?

他们是谁？
Tāmen shì shéi?
Who are they?

A

这是我妹妹。
Zhè shì wǒ mèimei.
This is my younger sister.

他们是我家人。
Tāmen shì wǒ jiārén.
They are my family members.

谁 can also be placed at the beginning of a sentence to act as the subject.

谁 是 ...... ?

Q

谁是你姐姐？
Shéi shì nǐ jiějie?
Who is your elder sister?

谁是美国人？
Shéi shì Měiguó rén?
Who is American?

A

她是我姐姐。
Tā shì wǒ jiějie.
She is my elder sister.

他是美国人。
Tā shì Měiguó rén.
He is American.

Part 3

Q 哪个①是你哥哥?
Nǎge shì nǐ gēge?
Which one is your elder brother?

A 我妈妈后边②的那个③人是我哥哥。
Wǒ māma hòubian de nàge rén shì wǒ gēge.
The person behind my mother is my elder brother.

Q 你哥哥右边④是谁?
Nǐ gēge yòubian shì shéi?
Who is the person to your elder brother's right?

A 我哥哥右边是我弟弟。
Wǒ gēge yòubian shì wǒ dìdi.
The person to my elder brother's right is my younger brother.

Q 中间⑤这个人是谁?
Zhōngjiān zhège rén shì shéi?
Who is the person in the middle?

A 中间这个人是我妹妹。
Zhōngjiān zhège rén shì wǒ mèimei.
The person in the middle is my younger sister.

Vocabulary

① 哪个 | *qw.*
nǎge | which;
which one

② 后边 | *n.*
hòubian | behind

③ 那个 | *pron.*
nàge | that;
that one

④ 右边 | *n.*
yòubian | right side

⑤ 中间 | *n.*
zhōngjiān | the middle

Language Notes

我妈妈后边
Wǒ māma hòubian

N. + PW.

By inserting a place word (PW) after the noun, we can specify the relative direction or location of someone and point out the person or item in that direction or at that location.

N. + PW. + 是…

▶ 我 妈 妈　　后 边　　　是　　我 弟弟。
Wǒ　māma　　hòubian　　shì　　wǒ　dìdi.

 The person behind my mother is my younger brother.

▶ 我 爸 爸　　右 边　　　是　　我 姐 姐。
Wǒ　bàba　　yòubian　　shì　　wǒ　jiějie.

The person to my father's right is my elder sister.

中 间 这 个 人
zhōngjiān zhège rén

PW. + N.

When the speaker knows the position of a person or an object, a place word can be placed in front of the noun to point out the specific direction or location.

PW. + N. + 是…

▶ 中 间　　　 这 个 人　　是　我 爸 爸。
Zhōngjiān　　zhège rén　　shì　wǒ bàba.

The person in the middle is my father.

▶ 左 边　　　 这 个 人　　是　我 妈 妈。
Zuǒbian　　 zhège rén　　shì　wǒ māma.

The person on the left is my mother.

Extra Information

In addition to 中间, we can also add 边, 面, 头 after prepositions such as 前, 后, 右, and 左 to form place words.

	前	后	右	左
边	前边 qiánbian	后边 hòubian	右边 yòubian	左边 zuǒbian
面	前面 qiánmiàn	后面 hòumiàn	—	—
头	前头 qiántou	后头 hòutou	—	—

Listening

1. Listen to David and Lily talk about their families. Read the statements below and choose true or false based on the conversation.

(1) T ☐ F ☐ 大卫家里有四口人。
Dàwèi jiālǐ yǒu sì kǒu rén.

(2) T ☐ F ☐ 大卫有一个哥哥。
Dàwèi yǒu yí ge gēge.

(3) T ☐ F ☐ 莉莉有一个哥哥和一个妹妹。
Lìli yǒu yí ge gēge hé yí ge mèimei.

(4) T ☐ F ☐ 莉莉家里有爸爸、妈妈、一个妹妹和她。
Lìli jiālǐ yǒu bàba māma yí ge mèimei hé tā.

(5) T ☐ F ☐ 莉莉家里有五口人。
Lìli jiālǐ yǒu wǔ kǒu rén.

2. Listen to the recording and choose the correct answer.

(1) a. 我家有七口人。 b. 我家有爷爷、奶奶、爸爸、妈妈、哥哥、弟弟和我。
Wǒ jiā yǒu qī kǒu rén.　　Wǒ jiā yǒu yéye、nǎinai、bàba、māma、gēge、dìdi hé wǒ.

c. 我没有兄弟姐妹。
Wǒ méiyǒu xiōng-dì-jiě-mèi.

(2) a. 是，她是我妈妈。　b. 这是我的书。　c. 她是我妈妈。
Shì, tā shì wǒ māma.　Zhè shì wǒ de shū.　Tā shì wǒ māma.

(3) a. 我爷爷后边是我奶奶。　b. 我奶奶后边是我爷爷。
Wǒ yéye hòubian shì wǒ nǎinai.　Wǒ nǎinai hòubian shì wǒ yéye.

c. 我爷爷右边是我奶奶。
Wǒ yéye yòubian shì wǒ nǎinai.

Matching

1. Look at May's family tree and answer the following questions in Chinese.

(1) 小美有几个兄弟姐妹?
   Xiǎoměi yǒu jǐ ge xiōng-dì-jiě-mèi?

   _____

(2) 小美家里有几口人?
   Xiǎoměi jiālǐ yǒu jǐ kǒu rén?

   _____

(3) 小美家里有什么人?
   Xiǎoměi jiālǐ yǒu shénme rén?

   _____

May (小美)

2. Draw your own family tree and answer the following questions in Chinese.

(1) 你家有几口人?
   Nǐ jiā yǒu jǐ kǒu rén?

   _____

(2) 你有几个兄弟姐妹?
   Nǐ yǒu jǐ ge xiōng-dì-jiě-mèi?

   _____

(3) 你家有什么人?
   Nǐ jiā yǒu shénme rén?

   _____

Choice

美美 (Měiměi) and a friend are looking at her family photo. Her friend has some questions about this photo. Please answer those questions as 美美.

(1) Q: 奶奶右边是谁？
　　　Nǎinai yòubian shì shéi?

　　美美：＿＿＿＿＿＿＿
　　Měiměi:

　　a. 我奶奶右边是我爷爷。
　　　 Wǒ nǎinai yòubian shì wǒ yéye.

　　b. 我奶奶右边是我弟弟。
　　　 Wǒ nǎinai yòubian shì wǒ dìdi.

　　c. 我奶奶右边是我哥哥。
　　　 Wǒ nǎinai yòubian shì wǒ gēge.

(2) Q: 哪个是你哥哥？
　　　Nǎge shì nǐ gēge?

　　美美：＿＿＿＿＿＿＿
　　Měiměi:

美美
Měiměi

　　a. 我爷爷后边的那个人是我哥哥。
　　　 Wǒ yéye hòubian de nàge rén shì wǒ gēge.

　　b. 我奶奶右边的那个人是我哥哥。
　　　 Wǒ nǎinai yòubian de nàge rén shì wǒ gēge.

　　c. 我妈妈後边的那个人是我哥哥。
　　　 Wǒ māma hòubian de nàge rén shì wǒ gēge.

(3) Q: 中间这个人是谁？
　　　Zhōngjiān zhège rén shì shéi?

　　美美：＿＿＿＿＿＿＿
　　Měiměi:

　　a. 中间这个人是我爸爸。
　　　 Zhōngjiān zhège rén shì wǒ bàba.

　　b. 中间这个人是我妈妈。
　　　 Zhōngjiān zhège rén shì wǒ māma.

　　c. 中间这个人是我。
　　　 Zhōngjiān zhège rén shì wǒ.

A Chance Encounter II

In this episode, we will introduce numbers and teach how to introduce one's family and ask about age.

Sentence Focus

Part 1　这是你的照片吗？

Part 2　他多大？他二十三岁。

　　　他是谁？他是我哥哥

Part 3　你有兄弟姊妹吗？你家有几口人？

林莉莉
Lín　Lìli
- 21 years old
- Sweet and easygoing
- Enjoys singing and cooking

王文正
Wáng　Wénzhèng
- 21 years old
- Energetic and smart
- Enjoys sports and movies

Part 1

CDR2-U4-P1

Lily is walking and looking at pictures and drops one. Wenzheng happens to be walking by and picks it up for her.

文正：
Wenzheng

Wenzheng:

莉莉！
Lìli!
Lily !

莉莉：
Lìli

Lily:

嗨！文正。早上好！
Hāi!　Wénzhèng.　Zǎoshàng hǎo!
Hi! Wenzheng. Good morning!

文正：

早上好！
Zǎoshàng hǎo!
Good morning!

文正：

这是你的照片[1]吗?
Zhèshì　nǐ　de zhàopiàn　ma?
Is this your picture?

莉莉：

是，这是我的。谢谢你！
Shì,　zhè shì wǒ de.　Xièxie nǐ!
Yes, it's mine. Thank you!

文正：

不客气。他们是你家人[2]吗?
Bú　kèqi.　Tāmen shì nǐ jiārén　ma?
You're welcome. Is this your family?

莉莉：

对，他们是我家人。
Duì,　tāmen shì wǒ jiārén.
Yes, this is my family.

Vocabulary

① 照片 | *n.*
zhàopiàn | picture

② 家人 | *n.*
jiārén | family members

Language Notes

的
de

的 is a possessive particle that normally follows a noun or pronoun. It functions like the possessive –'s in English.

你
nǐ

我
wǒ

他
tā

文 正
Wénzhèng

的
de

照片
zhàopiàn

Omitting 的
de

的 equals the possessive –'s in English. When two nouns have a close relationship, we can omit 的.

N1's + N2

Ex.

▶ 我(的)哥哥叫林 光中。
Wǒ (de)　gēge jiào Lín Guāngzhōng.
My elder brother's name is Guangzhong Lin.

▶ 我(的)家很大。
Wǒ (de) jiā hěn dà.
My house is very big.

Part 2

CDR2-U4-P2

Lily shows Wenzheng a picture and introduces her family.

莉莉:
Lìli
这是我爸爸，这是我妈妈。
Zhè shì wǒ bàba,　　zhè shì wǒ māma.

Lily:　　This is my father. This is my mother.

文正:
Wénzhèng
他是谁？
Tā shì shéi?

Wenzheng:　　Who is he?

莉莉:
他是我哥哥。
Tā shì wǒ gēge.

He is my brother.

文正:
他多❶大❷？
Tā duō dà?

How old is he?

莉莉:
他二十三岁❸。
Tā èrshísān suì.

He is twenty-three years old.

文正:
她是你妹妹吗？
Tā shì nǐ mèimei ma?

Is she your younger sister?

莉莉:
不是，她是我朋友❹。
Bú shì,　　tā shì wǒ péngyou.

No, she is my friend.

Vocabulary

❶ 多 duō | *qw.*
how (often used in an exclamatory sentence, such as "How much / many...")

❷ 大 dà | *sv.*
of age

❸ 岁 suì | *m.*
a year (of age)

❹ 朋友 péngyou | *n.*
friend

Language Notes

Asking one's age 多大 (duō dà) here means "how old." 多 is a question word that asks for an amount or degree to be clarified. When followed by a stative verb such as 大, the purpose of 多 is to ask about the extent of that stative verb.

S. + 多大?

Q 你多大?
Nǐ duō dà?
How old are you?

A 我 十八 岁。
Wǒ shíbā suì.
I'm eighteen years old.

王 文 正 多大?
Wáng Wénzhèng duō dà?
How old is Wenzheng Wang?

他 二十 一 岁。
Tā èrshíyī suì.
He is twenty-one years old.

Numbers

This is how we count from 1 to 10:

1	2	3	4	5	6	7	8	9	10
一	二	三	四	五	六	七	八	九	十
yī	èr	sān	sì	wǔ	liù	qī	bā	jiǔ	shí

This is how we count from 10 to 90:

10	20	30	40	50	60	70	80	90
十	二十	三十	四十	五十	六十	七十	八十	九十
shí	èrshí	sānshí	sìshí	wǔshí	liùshí	qīshí	bāshí	jiǔshí

In two-digit numbers, we add one number to 10, 20, and so on. Numbers in Chinese are similar to English in this regard. Here are some more examples, counting from 11–15 and then 26–29. Other two-digit numbers follow this rule, as well.

11	12	13	14	15
十一	十二	十三	十四	十五
shíyī	shí'èr	shísān	shísì	shíwǔ

26	27	28	29
二十六	二十七	二十八	二十九
èrshíliù	èrshíqī	èrshíbā	èrshíjiǔ

Part 3

Lily asks Wenzheng about his family.

莉莉:
Lìlì

文正，你有兄弟姐妹吗？

Wénzhèng, nǐ yǒu xiōng-dì-jiě-mèi ma?

Lily: Wenzheng, do you have brothers or sisters?

文正:
Wenzheng

有，我只有一个姐姐。

Yǒu, wǒ zhǐ yǒu yí ge jiějie.

Wenzheng: Yes. I only have an elder sister.

莉莉:

你家有几口人？

Nǐ jiā yǒu jǐ kǒu rén?

How many people are there in your family?

文正:

我家有六口人。

Wǒ jiā yǒu liù kǒu rén.

There are six people in my family.

莉莉:

一、二、三、四……

Yī、 èr、 sān、 sì…

One, two, three, four...

文正:

我家有爷爷、奶奶、爸爸、妈妈、姐姐和我。

Wǒ jiā yǒu yéye、 nǎinai、 bàba、 māma、 jiějie hé wǒ.

They are my grandfather, grandmother, father, mother, elder sister, and me.

Vocabulary

1 只
zhǐ | adv. | only

Language Notes

Measure Words

The measure word is a unique feature of Chinese. By inserting a measure word between the amount (number) and the noun, we categorize the noun. 岁 can be used as both a measure word and a noun, so adding another noun is unnecessary.

Nu. + M. + N.

Ex.

▶ 三 个 兄弟姐妹 — three siblings
sān / ge / xiōng-dì-jiě-mèi

▶ 六 口 人 — six people
liù / kǒu / rén

▶ 五 本 书 — five books
wǔ / běn / shū

▶ 二十一 岁 — twenty-one years old
èrshíyī / suì

几
jǐ

When 几 is used to form a question, it is followed by a measure word and a noun. 几 usually asks about a quantity that is assumed to be under ten.

几 + M. + N. ?

> * The phrase 几岁 (jǐ suì) can also be used to ask about someone's age. 几岁 has the same meaning as 多大 (duō dà). We generally use 几岁 to inquire about the age of children under ten.

Ex.

▶ 几 个 兄弟姐妹？
jǐ / ge / xiōng-dì-jiě-mèi?
How many siblings?

▶ 几 口 人？
jǐ / kǒu / rén?
How many people?

Q
你 有 几 本 书？
Nǐ yǒu jǐ běn shū?
How many books do you have?

你 几 岁？
Nǐ jǐ suì?
How old are you?

A
我 有 六 本 书。
Wǒ yǒu liù běn shū.
I have six books.

我 八 岁。
Wǒ bā suì.
I'm eight years old.

We Are a Family

CDR2 - U5

我是汤姆。
Wǒ shì Tāngmǔ.
My name is Tom.

我是玛莉。
Wǒ shì Mǎlì.
My name is Mary.

上 台 一 鞠躬。
Shàngtái yì jūgōng.
Let's take a bow.

今天我们来①说说「家庭②」。
Jīntiān wǒmen lái shuōshuo "jiātíng."
Today, we'll talk about "family."

嗯！说说「家庭」！
Ēn! Shuōshuo "jiātíng!"
Yep! Talk about "family."

你先说！
Nǐ xiān shuō!
You go first!

我们家是个大家庭。
Wǒmen jiā shì ge dà jiātíng.
We're a big family.

哦！大家庭！
Ó! Dà jiātíng!
有什么人呢？
Yǒu shénme rén ne?
Oh, a big family! Who are they?

我们家有爷爷、奶奶、
Wǒmen jiā yǒu yéye、 nǎinai、
外公、外婆、爸爸、
wàigōng、 wàipó、 bàba、
妈妈、哥哥、姐姐、
māma、 gēge、 jiějie、
弟弟、妹妹和我。
dìdi、 mèimei hé wǒ.

They are my paternal grandfather and grandmother,
maternal grandfather and grandmother, father,
mother, elder brother, elder sister, younger brother,
younger sister, and me.

慢点儿[3]！慢点儿！
Màn diǎnr!　　Màn diǎnr!
Slow down! Slow down!

哦！慢点儿是吧？
Ó!　　Màn diǎnr shì ba?
Oh! Slow down?

再来一次！
Zài lái yí cì!
Please repeat that!

我们家有爷爷、奶奶、
Wǒmen jiā yǒu yéye、　　nǎinai、

外公、外婆、爸爸、
wàigōng、　　wàipó、　　bàba、

妈妈、哥哥、姐姐、
māma、　　gēge、　　jiějie、

弟弟、妹妹和我。
dìdi、　　mèimei hé wǒ.

They are my paternal grandfather and grandmother, maternal grandfather and grandmother, father, mother, elder brother, elder sister, younger brother, younger sister, and me.

喝！好多哪！
Hè!　　Hǎo duō na!

有几口人呢？
Yǒu jǐ kǒu rén ne?

Oh! So many! How many are there?

有……爷爷、奶奶、
Yǒu…　　yéye、　　nǎinai、

外公、外婆、爸爸、
wàigōng、　　wàipó、　　bàba、

妈妈、哥哥、姐姐、
māma、　　gēge、　　jiějie、

弟弟、妹妹和我。有
dìdi、　　mèimei hé wǒ.　　Yǒu

十一口人！
shíyī kǒu rén!

There are . . . my paternal grandfather and grandmother, maternal grandfather and grandmother, father, mother, elder brother, elder sister, younger brother, younger sister, and me! There are eleven people.

喝！真是个大家庭！
Hè! Zhēn shì ge dà jiātíng!
What a big family!

你们家有几口人？
Nǐmen jiā yǒu jǐ kǒu rén?
How about your family?

我们家有五口人。
Wǒmen jiā yǒu wǔ kǒu rén.

我爸爸、我妈妈、
Wǒ bàba、 wǒ māma、

我哥哥、我姐姐和我。
wǒ gēge、 wǒ jiějie hé wǒ.

这是我们家的照片。
Zhè shì wǒmen jiā de zhàopiàn.

We have five people, including my father, mother, elder brother, elder sister, and me.
This is my family picture.

家庭照片。
Jiātíng zhàopiàn.
It's a family picture.

嗯，是。
Ēn, shì.
Yes, it is.

这是你爸爸？
Zhè shì nǐ bàba?
Is this your father?

这是我爸爸。
Zhè shì wǒ bàba.
This is my father.

那是你妈妈？
Nà shì nǐ māma?
Is that your mother?

那是我妈妈。
Nà shì wǒ māma.
That is my mother.

这……一定④是你哥哥！
Zhè … yídìng shì nǐ gēge!
This . . . must be your elder brother!

没错⑤！没错！
Méicuò! Méicuò!

他是我哥哥。
Tā shì wǒ gēge.

That's right! That's right! He's my elder brother.

这……女孩⑥是谁呀？
Zhè … nǚhái shì shéi ya?
Who is this girl?

她是我姐姐呀！
Tā shì wǒ jiějie ya!
She is my elder sister!

是你妹妹吧？
Shì nǐ mèimei ba?

Isn't she your younger sister?

我……才⑦是你弟弟呢！
Wǒ… cái shì nǐ dìdi ne!

I . . . AM your younger brother!

哟！乖⑧弟弟！弟弟乖！
Yō! Guāi dìdi! Dìdi guāi!

Well, my "good" younger brother! Be good,
my younger brother!

哎呀！天哪！
Àiya! Tiān na!

Oh my God!

我是汤姆。
Wǒ shì Tāngmǔ.

My name is Tom.

我是玛莉。
Wǒ shì Mǎlì.

My name is Mary.

下台一鞠躬。
Xiàtái yì jūgōng.

Let's take a bow.

Vocabulary

① 来 *v.* used before a verb to indicate that one is about to do something
lái

② 家庭 *n.* family
jiātíng

③ 慢点儿 *ce.* slow down a little bit
màn diǎnr

④ 一定 *adv.* certainly; indeed; surely
yídìng

⑤ 没错 *ce.* That's right!
méicuò

⑥ 女孩 *n.* girl
nǚhái

⑦ 才 *adv.* used to refute or top the previous speaker's statement
cái

⑧ 乖 *sv.* to be well-behaved; to be good
guāi

Extra Information

相声 (xiàngshēng, Chinese comic dialogue) is a traditional Chinese comedic performance. It is made up of four skills: speaking (说, shuō), imitating (学, xué), teasing (逗, dòu), and singing (唱, chàng). 相声 can be divided into a monologue, dialogue, and skit comedy, among which the dialogue aspect is usually the most popular.

Traditionally, 相声 follows a particular routine. When the performers are on the stage, they introduce themselves and bow to the audience, saying "上台一鞠躬 (shàngtái yì jūgōng)." Then, the show begins. When the show comes to an end, the performers give their names again, bow, and say "下台一鞠躬 (xiàtái yì jūgōng)."

Since 相声 is considered folk art, its language is more colloquial. In our lesson, we use many common interjections like 嗯 (ēn), 哦 (ó), 喝 (hè), 哎呀 (aiya), and 天哪 (tiān na) to make the language more natural.

Exercises

CDR2 - U5 - E

Listening

Look at the pictures below as you listen to the recording. Choose the answer that best fits the question you hear.

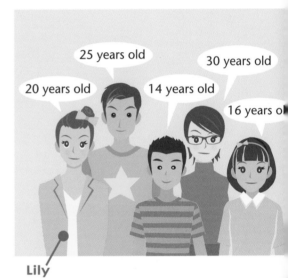

☐ (1) a. 有　　　 b. 没 有
　　　　yǒu　　　　 méiyǒu

☐ (2) a. 四 个　 b. 三 个　　 c. 两 个
　　　　sì ge　　　 sān ge　　　 liǎng ge

☐ (3) a. 二 十 五 岁 b. 二 十 三 岁　 c. 二 十 岁
　　　　èrshíwǔ suì　 èrshísān suì　 èrshí suì

☐ (4) a. 她 弟 弟　 b. 她 妹 妹　　 c. 她 姐 姐
　　　　tā dìdi　　 tā mèimei　　 tā jiějie

☐ (5) a. 她 弟 弟　 b. 她 妹 妹　　 c. 她 哥 哥
　　　　tā dìdi　　 tā mèimei　　 tā gēge

Choice

For questions 1–3, please choose a suitable answer from the ones provided in the box below. For 4–6, please choose the answer from the choices that follow the question.

a.请 再 说 一 次。	b.没错！	c.请 你 说 慢 点 儿！	d.你 先 说。
Qǐng zài shuō yí cì.	Méicuò!	Qǐng nǐ shuō màn diǎnr!	Nǐ xiān shuō.

☐ (1) This is your first Chinese class. What would you say if you wanted the teacher to speak a little slower?

☐ (2) What would you say to ask the teacher to repeat something?

☐ (3) In class, both you and a classmate raise your hands to answer a question. What would you say to let the other person speak first?

☐ (4) How would someone ask you your age?

    a. 你好吗?
       Nǐ hǎo ma?

    b. 你多大?
       Nǐ duō dà?

    c. 你是谁?
       Nǐ shì shéi?

☐ (5) How would you ask somebody if they had brothers or sisters?

    a. 你家有几口人?
       Nǐ jiā yǒu jǐ kǒu rén?

    b. 这是你哥哥吗?
       Zhè shì nǐ gēge ma?

    c. 你有兄弟姐妹吗?
       Nǐ yǒu xiōng-dì-jiě-mèi ma?

☐ (6) What would be a suitable answer to the above question?

    a. 我没有两个妹妹。
       Wǒ méiyǒu liǎng ge mèimei.

    b. 我有没有两个妹妹。
       Wǒ yǒu méiyǒu liǎng ge mèimei.

    c. 我有两个妹妹。
       Wǒ yǒu liǎng ge mèimei.

Ordering

1. Please put the following numbers in order and write the correct sequences below.

    (1) 一、三、二、五、四   _____

    (2) 十、十一、十五、十二、十四、十三 _____

    (3) 十、九、八、六、七   _____

2. Fill in the blanks to complete the sequence of numbers 1–10.

一、二、三、 ☐四 、 ☐ 、六、七、 ☐ 、 ☐ 、 ☐

Asking for Directions II

Part 1

Q 请问 _____ 在哪里？
Qǐngwèn   zài nǎlǐ?

Excuse me. Where is _____?

在故宫询问处 At the Information Center of the Palace Museum

Ex. 请问大门在哪里？
Qǐngwèn dàmén zài nǎlǐ?
Excuse me. Where is the entrance?

Or 请问售票处在哪里？
Qǐngwèn shòupiàochù zài nǎlǐ?
Excuse me. Where is the ticket office?

请问洗手间在哪里？
Qǐngwèn xǐshǒujiān zài nǎlǐ?
Excuse me. Where is the restroom?

请问公用电话在哪里？
Qǐngwèn gōngyòng diànhuà zài nǎlǐ?
Excuse me. Where is the public telephone?

请问小卖部在哪里？
Qǐngwèn xiǎomàibù zài nǎlǐ?
Excuse me. Where is the snack bar?

Give It a Try

售票处
shòupiàochù

ticket office

小卖部
xiǎomàibù

snack bar

餐厅
cāntīng

restaurant

公用电话
gōngyòng diànhuà

public telephone

洗手间
xǐshǒujiān

restroom

电梯
diàntī

elevator

Extra Information

Chinese has many different phrases that can refer to the restroom. 洗手间 (xǐshǒujiān), probably the most polite, literally means "a room for washing your hands." The phrase 厕所 (cèsuǒ) is also common, but among some people it is considered impolite. In mainland China, people also say 卫生间 (wèishēngjiān), which means "a room for personal hygiene." 盥洗室 (guànxǐshì) is often seen on signs, and women often use 化妆室 (huàzhuāngshì), as this refers to a place to do makeup.

unit
6

Sentence Patterns 中文句型

Part 2

CDR2 - U6 - P2

A

在询问处的＿＿＿＿＿。
Zài xúnwènchù de

＿＿＿＿＿＿＿＿ of the Information Center.

在故宫询问处 At the Information Center of the Palace Museum

Ex. 在询问处的前边。
Zài xúnwènchù de qiánbian.
It's in front of the Information Center.

Or 在询问处的后边。
Zài xúnwènchù de hòubian.
It's behind the Information Center.

在询问处的右边。
Zài xúnwènchù de yòubian.
It's on the Information Center's right.

在询问处的左边。
Zài xúnwènchù de zuǒbian.
It's on the Information Patern's left.

在询问处的对面。
Zài xúnwènchù de duìmiàn.
It's across from the Information Center.

94

Give It a Try

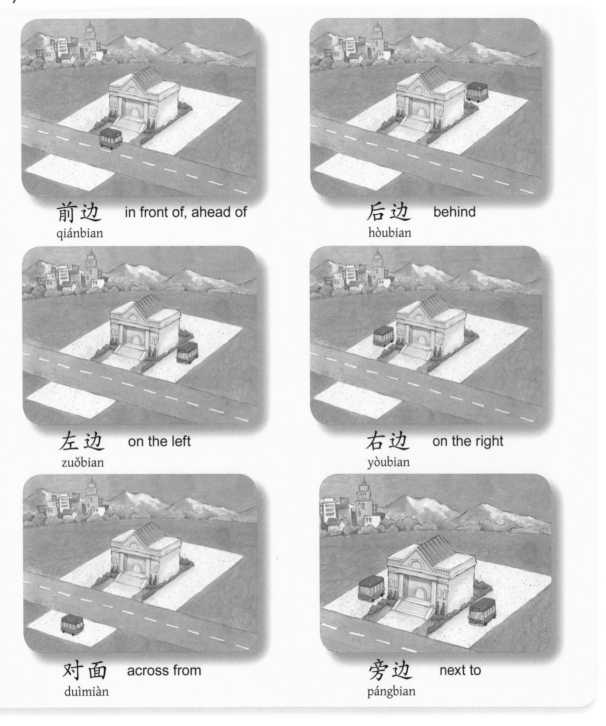

前边　in front of, ahead of
qiánbian

后边　behind
hòubian

左边　on the left
zuǒbian

右边　on the right
yòubian

对面　across from
duìmiàn

旁边　next to
pángbian

Extra Information

Most museums offer guided tours. If you want to join a guided tour, go to the 讲解服务处 (jiǎngjiě fúwù chù, guide service center). If you prefer to take your time and visit the museum by yourself, go to the 自动导游讲解器租机处 (zìdòng dǎoyóu jiǎngjiěqì zūjīchù, audio guide rental center) to rent an audio guide device. This way, you can listen to the narration at your own leisure.

Exercises

Matching

Match the pictures below with the phrases.

(1) 公 用 电 话
gōngyòng diànhuà

(2) 小 卖 部
xiǎomàibù

(3) 餐 厅
cāntīng

(4) 售 票 处
shòupiàochù

(5) 洗 手 间
xǐshǒujiān

(6) 电 梯
diàntī

a 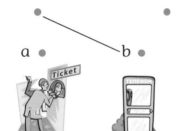   b    c   d   e   f

Listening

CDR2 - U6 - E

1. Listen to the recording and complete the dialogue.

☐ (1) Q: _____

A: a. 洗 手 间 在 大 门 的 前 边 。 b. 售 票 处 在 大 门 的 左 边 。
　　 Xǐshǒujiān zài dàmén de qiánbian.　　 Shòupiàochù zài dàmén de zuǒbian.

　　 c. 大 门 在 右 边 。
　　　 Dàmén zài yòubian.

☐ (2) Q: _____

A: a. 在 公 用 电 话 的 后 边 。 b. 公 用 电 话 在 大 门 的 后 边 。
　　 Zài gōngyòng diànhuà de hòubian.　　 Gōngyòng diànhuà zài dàmén de hòubian.

　　 c. 大 门 在 公 用 电 话 的 后 边 。
　　　 Dàmén zài gōngyòng diànhuà de hòubian.

☐ (3) Q: _____

A: a. 电 梯 前 边 是 电 话 。 b. 大 门 在 电 梯 旁 边 。
　　 Diàntī qiánbian shì diànhuà.　　 Dàmén zài diàntī pángbian.

　　 c. 电 梯 在 大 门 旁 边 。
　　　 Diàntī zài dàmén pángbian.

☐ (4) Q: a. 请 问 餐 厅 在 哪 里 ?
Qǐngwèn cāntīng zài nǎlǐ?

b. 请 问 售 票 处 在 哪 里 ?
Qǐngwèn shòupiàochù zài nǎlǐ?

c. 请 问 洗 手 间 在 哪 里 ?
Qǐngwèn xǐshǒujiān zài nǎlǐ?

A: _____

☐ (5) Q: a. 请 问 小 卖 部 在 哪 里 ?
Qǐngwèn xiǎomàibù zài nǎlǐ?

b. 请 问 询 问 处 在 哪 里 ?
Qǐngwèn xúnwènchù zài nǎlǐ?

c. 请 问 大 门 在 哪 里 ?
Qǐngwèn dàmén zài nǎlǐ?

A: _____

2. Please look at the picture and listen to the recording.

Word Bank: a. 小 卖 部   b. 洗 手 间   c. 公 用 电 话
xiǎomàibù   xǐshǒujiān   gōngyòng diànhuà

(1) Label each place with the corresponding letter from the word bank.

(2) Answer the following questions in Chinese.

Q: 餐厅在哪里?   A: _____
Cāntīng zài nǎlǐ?

Q: 售票处在哪里?   A: _____
Shòupiàochù zài nǎlǐ?

Q: 电梯在哪里?   A: _____
Diàntī zài nǎlǐ?

家 *and* 高

CDR2-U7

家 (jiā) combines the two pictographs 宀 (roof) and 豕 (pig). In ancient China, most households raised pigs as domestic animals. The image of a pig under a roof, therefore, stands for the "home" or "family." The word 高 (gāo) reflects the image of a tall building, and it means "tall" or "high."

Order

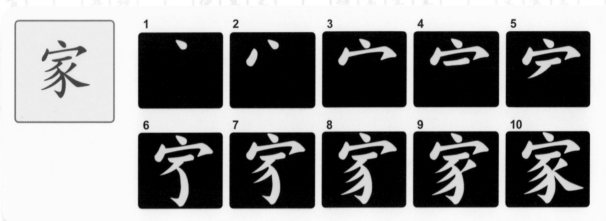

History

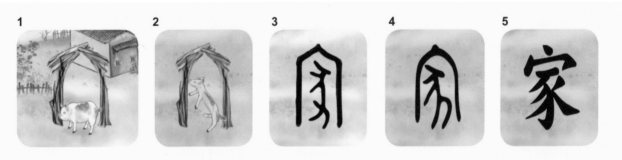

Examples

家	家庭	我 有 一 个 大 家 庭。
jiā	jiātíng	Wǒ yǒu yí ge dà jiātíng.
home; family	family	I have a big family.

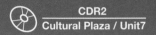
Order

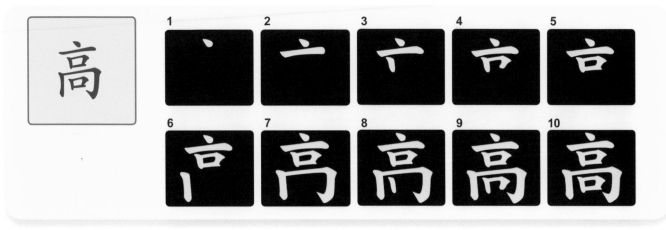

高

| 1 | 2 | 3 | 4 | 5 |
| 6 | 7 | 8 | 9 | 10 |

History

| 1 | 2 | 3 | 4 | 5 |

Examples

高
gāo

to be tall; to be high

高山
gāo shān

high mountain

中国有很多高山。
Zhōngguó yǒu hěn duō gāoshān.

There are many high mountains in China.

Give It a Try : Try to find and circle 家 and 高 in the following pictures.

Yum Cha & Ordering

Part 1 Dim Sum

一个芋头糕
yí　ge　yùtóugāo
one taro rice cake

六个芝麻球
liù　ge　zhīmáqiú
six fried sesame balls

两个荷叶珍珠鸡
liǎng ge　héyèzhēnzhūjī
two sticky rice
in lotus leaves

七个千层糕
qī　ge　qiāncénggāo
seven mille-layered
steamed cakes

三个春卷
sān ge chūnjuǎn
three fried spring rolls

八个豆沙包
bā　ge　dòushābāo
eight sweet red bean
Chinese steamed buns

四个烧卖
sì　ge　shāomài
four shaomai

九个叉烧酥
jiǔ　ge　chāshāosū
nine roasted pork buns

五个糖不甩
wǔ　ge　tángbùshuǎi
five rice balls with crushed
peanut

十个水饺
shí　ge　shuǐjiǎo
ten dumplings

Part 2 Ordering

请问 N 一 M 有几个？
Qǐngwèn   yī   yǒu jǐ ge?

Excuse me, how many N in one M ?

服务员： 欢迎光临，请问有几位？
Fúwùyuán
Huānyíng guānglín,   qǐngwèn yǒu jǐ wèi?

Waiter/
Waitress : Welcome, how many people in your party?

客人： 一位。
Kèrén
Yí wèi.

Customer : One.

服务员： 请问要点①什么？
Qǐngwèn yào diǎn shénme?

What would you like to order ?

客人： 我看看②。
Wǒ kànkan.

请问烧卖③一笼④有几个？
Qǐngwèn shāomài   yì lóng yǒu jǐ ge?

Let me see. How many shaomai are there in one basket?

服务员： 有四个。
Yǒu sì ge.

There are four.

客人： 水饺⑤一份⑥有几个？
Shuǐjiǎo yí fèn yǒu jǐ ge?

And how many dumplings are in one order ?

服务员： 一份有二十个。
Yí fèn yǒu èrshí ge.

There are twenty dumplings in one order .

Vocabulary

① 点 | v.
diǎn | to order

② 看看 | v.
kànkan | to have a look

③ 烧卖 | n.
shāomài | shaomai

④ 笼 | m.
lóng | a basket of

⑤ 水饺 | n.
shuǐjiǎo | dumpling

⑥ 份 | m.
fèn | a measure word for an order

客人： 我要两笼烧卖，
Wǒ yào liǎng lóng shāomài,

一份水饺。
yí fèn shuǐjiǎo.

I'd like two baskets of shaomai and one order of dumplings.

服务员： 好，请等一下。
Hǎo, qǐng děng yíxià.

OK, just a moment.

101

Exercises

Listening

Listen to the waitress and the customer talking at the restaurant. Choose the correct answer based on their conversation.

☐ (1) 有几位客人？
Yǒu jǐ wèi kèrén?

a. 一位　　　　b. 两位　　　　c. 三位
 yí wèi　　　　　liǎng wèi　　　　sān wèi

☐ (2) 水饺一份有几个？
Shuǐjiǎo yí fèn yǒu jǐ ge?

a. 三个　　　　b. 四个　　　　c. 十个
 sān ge　　　　　sì ge　　　　　shí ge

☐ (3) 烧卖一笼有几个？
Shāomài yì lóng yǒu jǐ ge?

a. 三个　　　　b. 五个　　　　c. 十个
 sān ge　　　　　wǔ ge　　　　　shí ge

☐ (4) 芝麻球一盘有几个？
Zhīmáqiú yì pán yǒu jǐ ge?

a. 两个　　　　b. 四个　　　　c. 十个
 liǎng ge　　　　sì ge　　　　　shí ge

☐ (5) 客人点了什么？ (There is more than one answer.)
Kèrén diǎnle shénme?

a. 烧卖　　　　b. 水饺　　　　c. 芝麻球　　　　d. 豆沙包
 shāomài　　　　shuǐjiǎo　　　　zhīmáqiú　　　　dòushābāo

Choice

Please fill in the blank with the corresponding letter that completes the conversation.

a. 请 问 要 点 什 么 Qǐngwèn yào diǎn shénme	b. 两 位 Liǎng wèi c. 我 看 看 Wǒ kànkan d. 有 五 个 Yǒu wǔ ge
e. 欢 迎 光 临 Huānyíng guānglín	f. 好 ， 请 等 一 下 Hǎo, qǐng děng yíxià g. 春 卷 一 盘 有 几 个 Chūnjuǎn yì pán yǒu jǐ ge

服 务 员 : _____ ！ 请 问 有 几 位 ？
Fúwùyuán: Qǐngwèn yǒu jǐ wèi?

客 人 : _____ 。
kèrén:

服 务 员 : _____ ？
Fúwùyuán:

客 人 : _____ 。 请 问 水 饺 一 份 有 几 个 ？
kèrén: Qǐngwèn shuǐjiǎo yí fèn yǒu jǐ ge?

服 务 员 ：有 二 十 个 。
Fúwùyuán: Yǒu èrshí ge.

客 人 : 烧 卖 一 笼 有 几 个 ？
kèrén: Shāomài yì lóng yǒu jǐ ge?

服 务 员 : _____ 。
Fúwùyuán:

客 人 : _____ ？
kèrén:

服 务 员 : 有 三 个 。
Fúwùyuán: Yǒu sān ge.

客 人 : 我 要 一 份 水 饺 ， 两 笼 烧 卖 ， 一 盘 春 卷 。
kèrén: Wǒ yào yí fèn shuǐjiǎo, liǎng lóng shāomài, yì pán chūnjuǎn.

服 务 员 : _____ 。
Fúwùyuán:

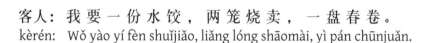

Tea Culture

Tea in Chinese Culture

In any reputable Chinese restaurant, a pot of hot tea will be on your table even before you start ordering. Tea is more than just a thirst quencher. Chinese people consider it to have social and cultural significance. For example, we offer tea to our guests to express gratitude, congratulations, or even an apology. Tea has been integrated into calligraphy, poetry, drama, and other literature since ancient times. Today, it is as closely linked to Chinese culture as it ever was.

Nowadays, similar to Western café culture, we drink tea at a so-called "teahouse" or "teateria" (from the word cafeteria). We can stay a good while, taking it easy and having a pot of tea with our friends. In some places, we can even enjoy live dance and music performances.

When you are having tea in a teahouse, you should take your time so that you can savor the color, flavor, and appearance of the tea you are drinking. Let's take a look at some of the more important tea preparation tools and go through the steps for making a good pot of tea.

茶壶 | teapot
cháhú

茶海 | serving pitcher
cháhǎi

茶杯 | teacup
chábēi

茶荷 | a container for fresh tea leaves
cháhé

烧水壶 | kettle
shāoshuǐhú

茶盘 | tea stand
chápán

茶匙 | tongs, to add and take tea leaves from the teapot
cháchí

How to Make Tea

1. Boil some water to preheat the teapot.

2. Fill the teapot one third full with tea leaves.

3. Rinse the tea leaves with hot water.

4. Pour boiling water into the pot one more time, allowing the water to overflow. Use the teapot lid to scrape any bubbles off the surface. Wait 30 seconds for the tea to brew.

5. Pour the tea into the serving pitcher. Use the serving pitcher to fill each teacup. Make sure the tea in every cup has a consistent color.

The Varieties of Tea

There are many types of Chinese tea. The teas have been classified as black tea, green tea, fixed green tea, white tea, yellow tea, and dark tea. They are also categorized based on their quality. There is even a "top ten list" for Chinese teas.

Listed below are several kinds of tea that are popular. They can be ordered in a teahouse or restaurant.

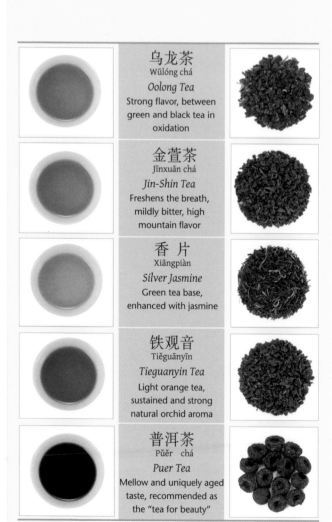

	乌龙茶 Wūlóng chá *Oolong Tea* Strong flavor, between green and black tea in oxidation	
	金萱茶 Jīnxuān chá *Jin-Shin Tea* Freshens the breath, mildly bitter, high mountain flavor	
	香 片 Xiāngpiàn *Silver Jasmine* Green tea base, enhanced with jasmine	
	铁观音 Tiěguānyīn *Tieguanyin Tea* Light orange tea, sustained and strong natural orchid aroma	
	普洱茶 Pǔěr chá *Puer Tea* Mellow and uniquely aged taste, recommended as the "tea for beauty"	

Listening

1. Listen to the recording and circle the finals you hear with the appropriate tone marks.

a	o	e	i	u	ü

(1) d ___ (i / ü)   (2) l ___ (u / ü)   (3) f ___ (e / o)   (4) w ___ (o / u)

(5) p ___ (a / o)   (6) y ___ (e / i)

2. Listen to the recording and write down the initials.

b	p	m	f	d	t	n
l	g	k	h	j	q	x
zh	ch	sh	r	z	c	s

(1) ___ ǎo   (2) ___ ǐ   (3) ___ ē   (4) ___ í

(5) ___ uī ___ ù   (6) ___ ǔ ___ ì

3. Listen to the recording and write down the finals with the appropriate tone marks.

ai	ei	ao	ou	an
en	ang	eng	er	

(1) h ___   (2) l ___   (3) f ___   (4) r ___

(5) w ___   (6) t ___

4. Listen to the recording and circle the initials you hear with the appropriate tone marks.

(1) ☐ ___ en (p / b)   (2) ☐ ___ i (d / t)   (3) ☐ ___ uan (k / g)   (4) ☐ ___ en (c / ch)

(5) ☐ ___ ang (s / sh)   (6) ☐ ___ ao (z / zh)   (7) ☐ ___ ue (j / z)   (8) ☐ ___ in (x / s)

5. You will hear a statement for each question. Choose the picture (A, B, or C) that best represents the situation in each statement.

(1) a.

b.

c.

(2) a.

b.

c.

(3) a.

b.

c.

(4) a.

b.

c.

(5) a. 　　　b. 　　　c.

(6) a. 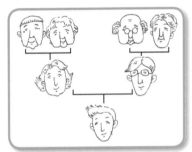　　　b. 　　　c.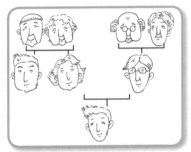

6. You will hear a sentence and see a picture for each question. Choose the best response (A, B, or C) in each instance.

(1)

a. 他很好。
　 Tā hěn hǎo.

b. 他不错。
　 Tā búcuò.

c. 他不太好。
　 Tā bú tài hǎo.

(2)

a. 你可以骑自行车到故宫
　 博物院。
　 Nǐ kěyǐ qí zìxíngchē dào
　 Gùgōng Bówùyuàn.

b. 你可以骑摩托车到故宫
　 博物院。
　 Nǐ kěyǐ qí mótuōchē dào
　 Gùgōng Bówùyuàn.

c. 你可以乘公交车到故宫
　 博物院。
　 Nǐ kěyǐ chéng gōngjiāochē
　 dào Gùgōng Bówùyuàn.

(3)

a. 他要一个碗。
　 Tā yào yí ge wǎn.

b. 他要筷子。
　 Tā yào kuàizi.

c. 他要一碗面。
　 Tā yào yì wǎn miàn.

(4)

a. 她骑摩托车到北京。
   Tā qí mótuōchē dào Běijīng.

b. 她乘公交车到北京。
   Tā chéng gōngjiāochē dào
   Běijīng.

c. 她乘地铁到北京。
   Tā chéng dìtiě dào Běijīng.

(5)

a. 他两岁。
   Tā liǎng suì.

b. 他二十五岁。
   Tā èrshíwǔ suì.

c. 他七十五岁。
   Tā qīshíwǔ suì.

(6)

a. 她最近很不错。
   Tā zuìjìn hěn búcuò.

b. 她最近不太好。
   Tā zuìjìn bú tài hǎo.

c. 她最近很好。
   Tā zuìjìn hěn hǎo.

7. You will hear a short dialogue. Choose the picture (A, B, or C) that best represents the situation in each dialogue.

(1) a.

b.

c.

(2) a.

b.

c.

(3) a.

b.

c.

(4) a.

b.

c.

8. You will hear a statement for each question. Choose the best response (A, B, or C) in each stance.

(1) a. 没关系。Méiguānxi.

b. 不客气。Bú kèqi.

c. 一会儿见。Yíhuìr jiàn.

(2) a. 明天很好。Míngtiān hěn hǎo.

b. 不客气。Bú kèqi.

c. 明天见。Míngtiān jiàn.

(3) a. 你可以乘出租车。Nǐ kěyǐ chéng chūzūchē.

b. 你可以到长城。Nǐ kěyǐ dào Chángchéng.

c. 你可以星期日走。Nǐ kěyǐ Xīngqīrì zǒu.

(4) a. 我不大。Wǒ bú dà.

b. 我十一岁。Wǒ shíyī suì.

c. 我有很多。Wǒ yǒu hěn duō.

(5) a. 他们是我朋友。Tāmen shì wǒ péngyou.

b. 他们叫王文正。Tāmen jiào Wáng Wénzhèng.

c. 他们有很多人。Tāmen yǒu hěn duō rén.

(6) a. 我家有人。Wǒ jiā yǒu rén.

b. 我家没有人。Wǒ jiā méiyǒu rén.

c. 我家有五口人。Wǒ jiā yǒu wǔ kǒu rén.

Choice

1. Each question has three statements. Choose the correct statement.

(1) a. 请问你是什么名字？
Qǐngwèn nǐ shì shénme míngzi?

b. 请问你叫什么名字？
Qǐngwèn nǐ jiào shénme míngzi?

c. 请问你的什么名字？
Qǐngwèn nǐ de shénme míngzi?

(2) a. 请说再一次。
Qǐng shuō zài yí cì.

b. 请再一次说。
Qǐng zài yí cì shuō.

c. 请再说一次。
Qǐng zài shuō yí cì.

(3) a. 大明，你先一下等。
Dàmíng, nǐ xiān yíxià děng.

b. 大明，你先等一下。
Dàmíng, nǐ xiān děng yíxià.

c. 大明，你一下先等。
Dàmíng, nǐ yíxià xiān děng.

(4) a. 莉莉，你家是什么人？
Lìli, nǐ jiā shì shénme rén?

b. 莉莉，你家有怎么人？
Lìli, nǐ jiā yǒu zěnme rén?

c. 莉莉，你家有什么人？
Lìli, nǐ jiā yǒu shénme rén?

2. Fill in the blanks. Choose the best answer to complete the sentence.

(1) 大明最近 _____ 错。
Dàmíng zuìjìn _____ cuò.

a. 不太   b. 还不   c. 还太
bú tài   hái bú   hái tài

(2) 你是 _____ 国人？
Nǐ shì _____ guó rén?

a. 哪   b. 什么   c. 谁
nǎ   shénme   shéi

(3) 他 _____ 日本人。
Tā _____ Rìběn rén.

a. 不是   b. 是不   c. 不
bú shì   shì bú   bù

(4) 那位先生是 _____ 的爷爷？
Nà wèi xiānsheng shì _____ de yéye?

a. 谁   b. 什么   c. 几
shéi   shénme   jǐ

(5) 你好，我们有八 _____ ，要点九 _____ 水饺。
Nǐ hǎo, wǒmen yǒu bā _____ , yào diǎn jiǔ _____ shuǐjiǎo.

a. 份，个   b. 位，份   c. 笼，位
fèn, ge   wèi, fèn   lóng, wèi

3. Read the statement and choose the picture that it best matches.

(1) 请给我刀子、叉子，谢谢！
Qǐng gěi wǒ dāozi、chāzi, xièxie!

a.

b.

c.

(2) 请问有牛肉面吗?
Qǐngwèn yǒu niúròumiàn ma?

a.

b.

c.

(3) 我家有爷爷、爸爸、妈妈、妹妹和我。
Wǒ jiā yǒu yéye、bàba、māma、mèimei hé wǒ.

a.

b.

c.

(4) 两本书是大山的，四本书是大山的朋友文正的。
Liǎng běn shū shì Dàshān de, sì běn shū shì Dàshān de péngyou Wénzhèng de.

a.

b.

c.
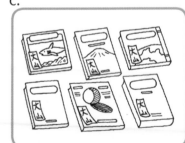

4. Please answer the questions and fill in the blanks from the box.

> a. 请问 qǐngwèn
> b. 不客气 bú kèqi
> c. 好久不见 hǎo jiǔ bú jiàn
> d. 请问您贵姓 qǐngwèn nín guìxìng
> e. 你好吗 nǐ hǎo ma
> f. 谢谢 xièxie
> g. 早上好 zǎoshàng hǎo
> h. 晚上好 wǎnshàng hǎo
> i. 明天见 míngtiān jiàn
> j. 对不起 duìbùqǐ

(1) What should you say when others say "Thank you"? _____

(2) What is a polite way to ask someone his/her surname? _____

(3) How do you politely start a question? _____

(4) What would you say if you bumped into someone? _____

(5) How do you greet people with "How are you?" in Chinese? _____

(6) How do you say "See you tomorrow"? _____

5. Look at the pictures and fill in the blanks with suitable expressions from the box.

> a. A：对不起！Duìbùqǐ!
>   B：没关系。Méiguānxi.
> b. A：谢谢！Xièxie!
>   B：不客气！Bú kèqi!
> c. A：请。Qǐng.
>   B：谢谢！Xièxie!
> d. A：再见！Zàijiàn!
>   B：再见！Zàijiàn!

Matching

1. Answer the following questions according to the information in the pictures.

(1) Korean

金大明 Jīn Dàmíng

Q1: 他姓什么?
Tā xìng shénme?

A1: _____

Q2: 他叫金吗?
Tā jiào Jīn ma?

A2: _____

Q3: 他是日本人吗?
Tā shì Rìběn rén ma?

A3: _____

(2) Chinese

王莉莉 Wáng Lín Lìli

Q1: 她姓林吗?
Tā xìng Lín ma?

A1: _____

Q2: 她叫莉莉吗?
Tā jiào Lìli ma?

A2: _____

Q3: 她是哪国人?
Tā shì nǎ guó rén?

A3: _____

(3) Japanese

小林文文   小林美美
Xiǎolín Wénwén   Xiǎolín Měiměi

Q1: 他们姓金吗?
Tāmen xìng Jīn ma?

A1: _____

Q2: 他们叫什么名字?
Tāmen jiào shénme míngzi?

A2: _____

Q3: 他们是韩国人吗?
Tāmen shì Hánguó rén ma?

A3: _____

2. Fill in the blanks with the Chinese expressions for different family members.

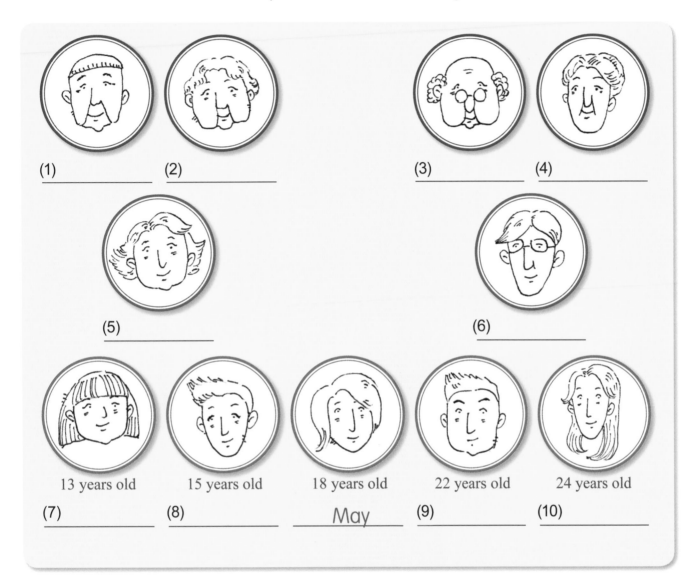

(1) _____ (2) _____   (3) _____ (4) _____

(5) _____   (6) _____

13 years old   15 years old   18 years old   22 years old   24 years old

(7) _____ (8) _____   May _____   (9) _____ (10) _____

3. Look at the pictures and fill in the blanks with nember and measure words.

birth date: 1988/6/30

(1) 他家有 _____ 人。   (2) 她有 _____ 书。   (3) 他多大?   (4) 他有 _____ 妹妹。

Tā jiā yǒu   rén.   Tā yǒu   shū.   Tā duō dà?   Tā yǒu   mèimei.

他今年 _____ 。
Tā jīnnián

4. A wants to go to the movies with friends, but he doesn't know where the theater is. He is asking a stranger (B) for help.

A: 不好意思，我想去看电影，请问 (1)_____?
   Bù hǎoyìsi, wǒ xiǎng qù kàn diànyǐng, qǐngwèn _____?

B: 电影院……。我们现在在邮局的 (2)_____，你知道火车站在哪里吗?
   Diànyǐngyuàn... wǒmen xiànzài zài yóujú de _____, nǐ zhīdào huǒchēzhàn zài nǎlǐ ma?

A: 我知道，它在邮局的 (3)_____。
   Wǒ zhīdào, tā zài yóujú de _____.

B: 对，火车站后面有 (4)_____，电影院就在它的 (5)_____。
   Duì, huǒchēzhàn hòumian yǒu _____, diànyǐngyuàn jiù zài tā de _____.

A: 好，我知道了，谢谢你！
   Hǎo, wǒ zhīdào le, xièxie nǐ!

5. According to the information in the pictures, answer the following questions.

(1) 滑板(skateboard)在餐厅的 _____。
   Huábǎn zài cāntīng de

(2) 我的朋友在餐厅的 _____。
   Wǒ de péngyou zài cāntīng de

(3) 学校在餐厅的 _____。
   Xuéxiào zài cāntīng de

(4) 电话在餐厅的 _____。
   Diànhuà zài cāntīng de

Answer Key 解答

Unit 1 Chinese Pronunciation

Listing

1. (1) gǒu   (2) yú   (3) shū

     (4) sǎn   (5) bǐ   (6) huā

     (7) cǎo   (8) shān

2. (1) Yes (táng, tuǐ)   (2) No (kǒu, gǒu)

     (3) No   (jī, zǐ)   (4) No (cǎo, chē)

     (5) Yes (fēi, fèi)   (6) No (xuě, xiě)

3. (1) `    (bù)    (2) ˇ (mǐ)    (3) ` (è)

     (4) — (fā)   (5) ′ (tíng)   (6) ′ (yún)

     (7) — (kuān)   (8) ′ (chéng)   (9) ˇ (zǐ)

Unit 2 Picture Dictionary

Choice

(1) a   (2) c   (3) b   (4) c   (5) a   (6) c

(7) c   (8) c   (9) b   (10) a

Unit 3 Useful Sentences

Choice

1. (1) b   (2) d   (3) c   (4) a

2. (1) b   (2) c

3. (1) ① a   ② b   ③ c   ④ a   ⑤ d

     (2) ① d   ② b   ③ a   ④ c   ⑤ c

Unit 5 Talk Show

Listening

(1) c   (2) a   (3) b

Choice

(1) b   (2) b   (3) c   (4) c   (5) b

Unit 6 Sentence Patterns

Matching

(1) a   (2) f   (3) e   (4) d   (5) c   (6) b

Choice

1. (1) c   (2) b   (3) a

2. (1) a   (2) c   (3) c

Unit 7 Asian Attractions

Choice

1. (1) e   (2) h   (3) d   (4) f   (5) c

     (6) b   (7) a   (8) g

2. (1) b   (2) a   (3) c   (4) a

3. d, a, c, e, f, b

Unit 1 Chinese Pronunciation

Listening

1. (1) 灯(dēng) / 疼(téng) (2) 早(zǎo) /找(zhǎo)

     (3) 西(xī) /四(sì)   (4) 冰(bīng) / 瓶(píng)

     (5) 擦(cā) / 茶(chá)

2. (1) g (gǔ)   (2) sh (shǒu)   (3) q (qiú)

     (2) x (xié)

3. (1) jù zhù   (2) suān shuān

     (3) zhào zào   (4) qiàn càn

4. (1) wan   (2) mangren   (3) lanqiu

     (4) nühai   (5) toufa

5. (1) d (a. yí   b. yú   c. lǔ   d. lú)

     (2) ab (a. lán   b. lóu   c. nán d. nuó)

     (3) acd (a. ēnhuì   b. ānhuì   c. ménfáng

         d. rénlèi)

     (4) bcd (a. fángshè   b. huángsè   c. jiéhūn

         d. huīhuáng)

6. (1) a (a. tōu   b. dōu   c. tuō   d. duō)

     (2) d (a. rù   b. wù   c. nù   d. hù)

     (3) b (a. huáng   b. huán   c. fáng   d. fán)

     (4) d (a. xǔyuàn   b. xǐyuàn   c. xǔyàn

         d. xǐyàn)

Unit 2 Picture Dictionary

Matching

1. (1) g   (2) a   (3) d   (4) h   (5) c   (6) b

2. (1) c   (2) a   (3) b   (4) d   (5) a

     (6) f   (7) d   (8) c   (9) e   (10) b

Unit 3 Useful Sentences

Listening
1. (1) T (2) T (3) F (4) F (5) T
2. (1) b (2) c (3) a

Matching
(1) 小美有两个姐妹，一个姐姐，一个妹妹
(2) 小美家有七口人
(3) 爷爷、奶奶、爸爸、妈妈、姐姐、妹妹和小美

Choice
(1) a (2) a (3) b

Unit 5 Talk Show

Listening
(1) a (2) a (3) c (4) a (5) a

Choice
(1) c (2) a (3) d (4) b (5) c (6) c

Ordering
1. (1) 一、二、三、四、五、六
(2) 十、十一、十二、十三、十四、十五
(3) 六、七、八、九、十
2. 五、八、九、十

Unit 6 Sentence Patterns

Matching
1. b **2.** d **3.** e **4.** a **5.** f **6.** c

Listening
1. (1) a (2) b (3) c (4) b (5) a
2. (1) ① a ② b ③ c

Unit 8 Asian Attractions

Listening
1. a **2.** c **3.** b **4.** a **5.** b, c

Choice
1. e, b, a, c, d, g, f

Review

Listening
1. (1) i , ` (2) ü , ˇ (3) o , ´ (4) u , ´
(5) a , — (6) e , ´
2. (1) t (2) d (3) k (4) p (5) h; f
(2) n ; l
3. (1) ai , ` (2) an , ´ (3) eng , —
(4) ou , ` (5) ēn (6) āng
4. (1) b , ˇ (2) t , — (3) k , — (4) ch , ` (5) sh , —
(6) z , ˇ (7) j , ´ (8) x , —
5. (1) b (2) c (3) b (4) c (5) b (6) a
6. (1) c (2) a (3) c (4) a (5) b (6) b
7. (1) b (2) b (3) a (4) c
8. (1) b (2) c (3) a (4) b (5) a (6) c

Choice
1. (1) b (2) c (3) b (4) c
2. (1) b (2) a (3) a (4) a (5) b
3. (1) c (2) b (3) c (4) b
4. (1) b (2) d (3) a (4) j (5) e (6) i
5. (1) d (2) c (3) b (4) a

Matching
1. (1) A1: 他姓金。
A2: 不，他叫大明。
A3: 他不是日本人，他是韩国人。
(2) A1: 不，她不姓林，她姓王。
A2: 是，她叫莉莉。
A3: 她是中国人。
(3) A1: 不，他们不姓金,他们姓林。
A2: 他们叫文文、美美。
A3: 不，他们不是韩国人，他们是日本人。
2. (1) 外公（姥爷） (2) 外婆 (3) 爷爷 (4) 奶奶 (姥姥)
(5) 妈妈 (6) 爸爸 (7) 妹妹 (8) 弟弟
(9) 哥哥 (10) 姐姐
3. (1) 四口 (2) 三本 (3) 二十岁 (4) 两个
4. (1) 电影院在哪里 (2) 前边 (3) 后边 (4) 百货公司
(5) 右边
5. (1) 左边 (2) 右边 (3) 后边 (4) 前边

Award-Winning Chinese Learning Products
That You Absolutely Must Have

The U.S.'s 7th Annual *Horizon Interactive Award: Bronze Winner*

ORDER NOW!

Live Interactive Chinese:

Employs innovative multimedia techniques to teach Chinese in a comprehensive way. Includes an illustrated dictionary, practical dialogs, a breakdown of Chinese characters, *and more!*

24 Themes: Speak Chinese Step-by-Step

Basic Chinese
1. Greetings and Introductions
2. My Family
3. Food
4. Hobbies
5. Phone Conversation
6. Making an Appointment
7. Emotions
8. Transportation

Applied Chinese
9. Travel
10. Shopping
11. Sports and Recreation
12. Studying Abroad
13. Survival Chinese
14. Social Life
15. Everyday Usage
16. Chinese Culture and festival

Business Chinese
17. Job Interviews
18. Office Chinese
19. Business Phone Calls
20. Meetings
21. Business Arrangements
22. Presentations
23. Negotiations
24. Business Travel

Topics are subject to change.

* **From Vol. 1-8, we have two editions for you to choose from:**
  Simplified Chinese Edition: 1 Book + 1 Audio CD + 1 Interactive CD-ROM / MP3
  Traditional Chinese Edition: 1 Book + 1 Audio CD + 1 Interactive CD-ROM / MP3
* **From Vol. 9-24, the two editions are merged.**
  The Simplified + Traditional Edition includes: 1 Book + 1 Audio CD + 1 Interactive CD-ROM/MP3
* **Tutorial DVDs for each volume are also available.**

Chinese Pronunciation:

Introduces Hanyu Pinyin, tones, and how to combine sounds together.
The interactive CD-ROM also presents video demonstrations and practice exercises.

Set Includes:
Book + Interactive CD-ROM with MP3 files + Audio CD x 2

Illustrated Chinese-English Dictionary:

Features more than 1800 words with pictures, categorized into 15 different themes, i.e. at home, around town, hobbies, cultural insights and much more!

Set Includes:
Book + Interactive CD-ROM with MP3 files+ 3 Audio CDs

Kids Interactive Chinese:

Follow space alien Chidodo on a 3-D adventure around the house! With his guidance, kids will enjoy exploring and learning all about household vocabulary in Chinese.

Set Includes:
Storybook + Workbook + 2 Audio CDs + 2 Interactive CD-ROMs + Teacher's Guide

Illustrated Chinese-English Vocabulary Posters:

10 vocabulary posters (20" x 30") feature colorful illustrations with corresponding Chinese words in both simplified and traditional characters.

Topics Include:
❶ In the living room ❷ Emotions ❸ Fast food restaurant ❹ Chinese cuisine ❺ On the road ❻ Hobbies ❼ Campus ❽ In the classroom ❾ Sports ❿ Holidays

LiveABC
Leading Multimedia Learning in Chinese

LiveABC Interactive Corporation   **The U.S.** Tel: +1-909-869-6091   Fax: +1-626-956-0663   145 Brea Canyon Road #A4, Walnut, CA, 91789
Taiwan: Tel:+886-2-2578-2626   Fax:+886-2-2578-5800   12F, No.32, Sec. 3, Bade Road, Songshan, Taipei 105
Website: http://www.liveabc.com/english   **Email:** Chinese@liveabc.com

CD-ROM for Windows

To install:

Insert the CD-ROM into your CD-ROM drive. The CD-ROM will start automatically. When using the CD-ROM for the first time, select **Install**. The program will automatically set up *Microsoft Speech SDK 5.1*, *Microsoft Speech SDK 1 Language Pack*, and *Practice Makes Perfect: Beginning Chinese, Interactive Edition I* (or *II*, depending on disk). Click **OK**, then click **Install** and **Exit Setup**. Click on **Continue** to add items to a Program Group, and when the setup is complete, click **Run** to start the program. For subsequent use, simply click **Instant Install** on the main menu to use the CD-ROM.

If the program does not start automatically, double-click on MY COMPUTER; find and open your CD-ROM disk drive, then double click on the **AutoRun.exe** icon. Follow the instructions for installing on your hard drive.

Minimum System Requirements:

Computer: Windows XP and Vista or above
(Note: Speech recognition engine may not function in Vista)
Pentium 4 CPU
256 MB RAM (512 MB recommended)
CD-ROM Drive
16-bit color or above
Sound Card, Speaker, and Microphone
500 MB of available hard-disk space
Microsoft Media Player 9.0 or above

Chinese Script:

If Chinese script does not appear correctly on the CD-ROM, go to **Control Panel** on your computer and double click on **Regional and Language Options**. Select the **Languages** tab and click on **Install files for East Asian Languages**, then **OK**. Click **OK** to the pop-up window "Install Supplemental Language Support" and restart the computer.

Help:

See pages vii–viii of this book for more information on How to Use the CD-ROM.
The "Help" option on the CD-ROM menu also provides a detailed description of all the features, functions, and activities on the CD-ROM, including Recording, Role-Playing, Speech Recognition, and Editing Vocabulary Lists.

MP3 Files

The CD-ROM disks both contain all the MP3 audio recordings that accompany the book, so you can download them from either disk.
To download: Double-click on MY COMPUTER, find and open your CD-ROM disk drive by double-clicking on the PMP Beginning Chinese icon. Drag the folder "PMP BgCh MP3 Files" to your desktop.
The MP3 files can be played on your computer and loaded onto your MP3 player. For optimum use on the iPod:

1. Open iTunes on your computer.
2. Drag folder "PMP BgCh MP3 Files" into Music Library in the iTunes menu.
3. Sync your iPod with iTunes and eject iPod.
4. Locate recordings on your iPod by following this path:
   Main menu: **Music**
   Music menu: **Artists**
   Artist menu: **PMP Beginning Chinese**
   Album menu: **PMP Beginning Chinese: Part I**
   　　　　　　　PMP Beginning Chinese: Part II

Call 800-722-4726 if the CD-ROMs are missing from this book.
For technical support go to
http://www.mhprofessional.com/support/technical/contact.php